TEACHING THE INTERNET TO LIBRARY STAFF AND USERS

10 READY-TO-GO WORKSHOPS THAT WORK

BY WILLIAM D. HOLLANDS

NEAL-SCHUMAN NETGUIDE SERIES

NEAL-SCHUMAN PUBLISHERS, INC.

NEW YORK LONDON

Published by Neal-Schuman Publishers, Inc.
100 Varick Street
New York, NY 10013

Printed and bound in the United States of America.

Library of Congress Cataloging-in-Publication Data

Hollands, William D.
    Teaching the Internet to library staff and users : 10 ready-to-go workshops that work / William D. Hollands.
      p.   cm. -- (Neal-Schuman netguide series)
    Includes bibliographical references and index.
    ISBN 1–55570–349–6
    1. Computer network resources—Study and teaching (Continuing education)—United States.   I. Title   II. Series.
ZA4201.H65   1999
025.04'071—dc21   98–49488
                                                                              CIP

Contents

Acknowledgments

I would like to thank my friends and colleagues at the University of Michigan, the New York Public Library, and Microsoft Corporation for all they have taught me about librarianship and the Internet. Also the patrons at the libraries where I have worked: I learned more about training from them than from any book or manual. Thanks to my family and friends around the country for all their love and support, especially my mother and father. And thanks mostly, of course, to John, to whom this and all things in the future are dedicated.

Preface

Libraries are going online in droves. According to the *1997 National Survey of U.S. Public Libraries and the Internet*,* approximately 72 percent of all public libraries have some type of Internet connection (up from 44 percent in 1996 and 21 percent in 1994). The vast majority of libraries with Internet connections provide some type of access to the public. These two trends (increased connectivity, increased public access) will surely continue.

Because homes are not nearly so well connected as libraries, many people do not have Internet access anywhere other than through a library. While continuing to attract their current patrons, libraries have clearly found new customers who pass through their doors solely for Internet access. And the Internet offers libraries the potential for even more business: as Internet cafes and other public access points for online surfing die out, people are lining up to use library computers.

While library use and visibility is up, the Internet also presents libraries with enormous public service challenges. The public is exposed to a constant barrage of conflicting messages about the Internet: it's scary, it's dangerous, it's confusing. In order to attract and retain new Internet-savvy patrons, without alienating any of their original client bases, libraries must provide a range of services that go along with Internet access. Perhaps the most important of these services is training.

Libraries, like most other types of organizations, have learned (sometimes the hard way) that it is not enough to unload a truckload of new machines, hook them up, and throw open the lab doors. Ongoing support and training

---

* Bertot, John, et al. *The 1997 National Survey of U.S. Public Libraries and the Internet: Final Report.* American Library Association Office for Information Technology Policy, 1997. 4 July 1998
<http://www.ala.org/oitp/research/plcon97sum/> and
<http://research.umbc.edu/~bertot/ala97.html>.

are essential. For libraries, this training is necessary not only for patrons, but also for staff.

Teaching the Internet to Library Staff and Users: 10 Ready-To-Go Workshops That Work is a practical guide for librarians wishing to establish or refine ongoing Internet training for staff members or patrons. The primary audience is librarians and training coordinators, but anyone with responsibility for Internet training in libraries should find it relevant to their role. The book features ten customizable, ready-to-run workshops.

HOW TO USE THESE WORKSHOPS IN YOUR LIBRARY

Each workshop in this book includes an introduction, an objective, a timed lesson plan, tips, a sample script, and reproducible handouts. The sample scripts are presented to "flesh out" the lesson plan and to provide you with language that is easily adaptable to a variety of styles and needs; they should not be read verbatim during the training session.

Every attempt has been made to make the training modules in *Teaching the Internet to Library Staff and Users* as universally replicable as possible in terms of content, setting, and software. Naturally, though, some local customization is desirable. For example, elements of different workshops may be mixed and matched. In order to provide for the variety of settings librarians work in, the sample workshops are set in different training environments (computer lab, lecture room, etc.). The ten customizable workshops are:

Internet Train the Trainers (Part 1, Part 2, Part 3): A three-part series to train library staff members in sound Internet training principles and practices they can use with patrons.

Getting Started on the World Wide Web: An introduction to the World Wide Web, designed as a small-group demonstration for patrons.

Using Search Engines and Finding Information on the Web: A hands-on workshop focusing on Internet search engines and subject directories.

Books and Literature on the Web: A hands-on introduction to book and literature information on the Web, with an emphasis on current and popular fiction. As well as serving as a ready-to-go workshop, this can also be used as a model for other single-topic hands-on workshops.

College Information on the Web: A demonstration workshop about higher-education resources on the Web. This plan can also be used as a model for other single-topic demonstration workshops.

Introduction to HTML (Part 1, Part 2, Part 3): A three-part, hands-on introduction to basic HTML.

Before actually presenting any of the workshops, trainers will want to read through the entire lesson plan and sample script, several times. Then, you will want to make a copy of the lesson plan for yourself (either a photocopy or your own notes on notecards), making any necessary adjustments and additions. You will need to make enough copies of the handouts for your trainees. I urge you to practice the entire lesson by yourself at least once—out loud. This will help familiarize you with the material, give you a better sense of timing, and make you aware of any awkward spots that need more work. In your practice runs, actually perform the searches and demonstrations; again, this will give you a more realistic picture of how long they take and will make you more confident when you do them in the actual session. It is also a good idea to redo the searches immediately before the session, in case anything has changed. In terms of time, expect the actual session to take longer than your practice session.

Then, when you conduct the training, have a good time; you should feel confident because you are well prepared. Your enthusiasm and energy will transfer to your audience, and your confidence will set them at ease.

Finally, please use *Teaching the Internet to Library Staff and Users* primarily as a starting point. Develop your own workshops and tutorials using its guidelines and its models. Watch how your patrons use this incredible information resource, listen to their questions, and be prepared to respond with new kinds of instruction and training to help them make the most of their time online, and in the library.

Introduction

THE NEED FOR ONGOING INTERNET TRAINING

Due to the increasing prevalence—and popularity—of information technologies, libraries must train both existing and newly hired staff members in new technologies. This training may be focused on "competencies" that all employees must meet. However, perhaps more importantly, ongoing training creates a committed team of technology advocates—staff members who are comfortable with the technology, eager to keep their skill sets current, aware of technology's importance, and capable of integrating it into all their work routines and programs. Moreover, one cannot expect staff members to train clients if they have not been adequately trained themselves.

Today's opportunities can foster a new (or, rather, evolutionary) role for librarians: that of the trainer. Librarians, of course, have always been "trainers." Book talks, bibliographic instruction, and reference services are all educational or training activities; librarians do them every day, and have for years. The role of "technology trainer" will not evolve naturally, however. Training, particularly technology training, is a skill that must be learned; while some people are better suited to being trainers than others (and perhaps not everyone on staff should become a trainer), learning to be an effective trainer requires dedicated support and training.

Luckily, librarianship is full of professionals with the desire to educate and a good knowledge of information and information-seeking behavior. Thus the profession is particularly well suited to produce technology trainers. While librarians are doing this, they need ongoing support, and libraries must commit to providing this training and support to staff in order to build a dedicated team of technology advocates and trainers.

Teaching the Internet can be greatly rewarding. It is one of the best ways to come in close contact with clients and make a difference in their lives. Patrons are almost always overwhelmingly appreciative of technology training efforts. This vital role will help keep libraries positioned to be the information centers for their various communities, where Internet access and training is a large part of the mix. Moreover, there is no "end" in sight—no time when everyone will have all the training they need, nor when they will have access to all the information resources they can use at home or work. There will always be new content and new technology driving the need for more training.

A FEW BASIC TECHNOLOGY TRAINING PRINCIPLES

Most of the general training principles ascribed to and demonstrated in the training modules here are outlined in the Internet Train the Trainers workshops (Chapters 1-3). A list of resources for trainers can be found there, too. I will just highlight a few points here.

Training should be action-oriented. I have sat through many workshops where, having spent thousands of dollars to set up a computer lab, the trainer lectured for most of the session. After five minutes, the trainees started to fidget in their seats. After ten, they were either asleep or were looking longingly at their computer keyboards. The trainer had lost them.

Most of us learn best by doing. This is true for any training setting—a computer lab, a lecture hall, a small-group demonstration, or a one-on-one tutorial. Involve the participants, get them talking, questioning, and doing. Activity is a great trigger to memory. Moreover, actually performing a task does wonders for the confidence, and building confidence is a large part of what training should be about. Good training also inspires learners to continue learning on their own.

Good training also provides lasting encouragement. It is rare that anyone will remember more than a very few points from any single lecture or training session for very long. What can be memorable is a teacher's or trainer's encouragement and enthusiasm. Again, I have been in many training sessions where the trainer was extremely knowledgeable; he or she tried to pack as much of this knowledge as possible into the allotted time. This tendency is particularly common in technology and Internet-related training sessions. For example, Internet trainers have an unfortunate tendency to include details about the history and the technological underpinnings of the Internet—interesting information perhaps, but inappropriate for a room full of people who are just starting to learn to use the Web.

Usually, a trainer has a group of people for an hour, maybe two—not a lot of time. This is just enough time to generate a keen interest in the subject matter, to instill confidence, and to have the trainees perform a few fundamental tasks successfully. If you are successful in doing that, then your trainees will have the tools and the desire to continue exploring and learning on their own.

So, keep training simple, make it active, and (most importantly) spread your enthusiasm.

Chapter 1
Internet Train
the Trainers
(Part 1)

*Handouts for this workshop
follow page 33.*

OVERVIEW

Who

The audience for this workshop is library system employees (librarians and/or non-librarians) who will be conducting Internet training sessions for their patrons. They do not all work in the same branch but are scattered throughout the system. Some staff members will conduct Internet training sessions in the central computer lab where this training is taking place; others will conduct training sessions for smaller groups in their local branches, where they will gather around one or two computers. Some have volunteered to be Internet trainers; others have been assigned this duty. They all have a basic understanding of the Internet and the World Wide Web; beyond that, experience and knowledge vary.

What

This customizable, ready-to-run series of three workshops (see also Chapters

Some of the key concepts and activities in the "Internet Train the Trainers" workshop series (Chapters 1, 2, and 3) were adapted from the workshop and handbook *Training the Trainer*, written and presented by Beverly Hyman, 1995. (Presented at the American Management Association, New York City, NY, February 1997).

2 and 3) is an introduction to good training principles and practices, applied to Internet training for patrons of a large public library system. It can be adapted easily to smaller public libraries or library systems, as well as to academic and special libraries. While the focus is on providing effective Internet training, the principles covered can be applied to any kind of training, particularly technology training. Part 1 provides an introduction to the series, and covers some basic principles of effective training and adult learning.

Where

This workshop is designed for a computer lab with space for ten students and an instructor (eleven PCs with Internet access, one with projection for the instructor). This computer lab is also used for public training sessions; some of the students will conduct their Internet training sessions here. However, this workshop could be adapted to another setting (such as a larger lab, a lecture hall, or a room with one PC); in fact, it is not necessary that the first two sessions take place in the computer lab. This training is designed so that students can apply what they learn to whatever training setting is realistic for them.

When

This workshop is one hour and 20 minutes. All three sessions in the series should be required and completed in sequence; the trainees should complete the sessions as a group, if possible.

Why

This three-part series can help develop a cadre of Internet trainers so that a library or library system can provide ongoing Internet education for all staff and users without hiring outside experts. The objectives of this series are for the trainees to be able to (1) explain basic principles of learning; (2) apply those principles to the design of solid Internet training sessions for their patrons; and (3) conduct effective Internet training sessions with confidence.

The objectives for Part 1 are for the trainees to be able to (1) recognize effective training from the trainee's point of view; (2) explain basic principles of adult learning; and (3) write useful training objectives.

In addition, there are unstated objectives and side benefits to this three-part series. The review of the model "Introduction to the World Wide Web" workshop can serve to fill in gaps of knowledge among the employee-trainees. Also, the practice presentations will be varied in scope; inevitably, everyone will learn at least one thing about the Internet that he or she didn't know before.

Finally, another unstated objective is to get all of the trainees (or at least as many as possible) to buy into a public Internet training program and to feel enthusiastic about it. There may be resistance of various kinds to work through: fear of public speaking, fear of technology, apathy, stress and workload levels, or disagreement with the idea of a public training program itself.

BEFORE THE SESSION

Training packets should be sent to the participants about a week beforehand, with an introductory letter and directions to the computer lab, if necessary.

- The handouts for this series (see pages 34–44)
- A written agenda for the three-part "Internet Train the Trainers" series
- The model "Getting Started on the World Wide Web" workshop in Chapter 4
- Possibly a recent article of interest, such as one about effective use of search engines
- Name tags, if attendees do not know each other.

The letter should instruct everyone to review the model "Getting Started on the World Wide Web" workshop prior to the first session. The letter should also instruct everyone to bring their packets to every session.

WORKSHOP AGENDA

This lesson plan is crowded, so it is important to maintain control of this class. At the same time, one of the unstated objectives is to motivate the staff and get them to be enthusiastic about the public training program. Therefore, you want to encourage them to talk and to share their knowledge and experience. This should be easy: many of them will have experience in training, teaching, and/or bibliographic instruction. All of them will be experienced in helping patrons use the library and its resources. There can be some wonderful sharing in this three-part program, where everyone learns from each other. Be enthusiastic, be reassuring, and treat everyone as experienced equals; you as the trainer will learn as much from them as they do from you. The outline of the workshop follows.

Outline of Lesson

INTRODUCTION/OBJECTIVES (0:00–0:15)

- Welcome and introductions
- Participants' objectives for three-part series
- Trainer's objectives for three-part series: Trainees will be able to:
  1. Explain principles of learning
  2. Apply those principles to the design of solid Internet training sessions
  3. Conduct effective Internet training sessions with confidence.

AGENDA FOR THREE-PART SERIES: REVIEW (0:15–0:20)

REVIEW PACKET (0:20–0:25)

SAMPLE INTRODUCTION TO THE WORLD WIDE WEB: DISCUSSION (0:25–0:30)

- Strengths
- What could be done differently

TRAINING OVERVIEW (0:30–0:40)

- From trainee's point of view
- Measurable, observable, behavioral change
- Controlled by trainer

LEARNING PRINCIPLES (0:40–0:55)

- Action
- Association
- Resistance
- Simplicity
- Variety

TRAINING OBJECTIVES (0:55–1:10)

- Specific
- Attainable
- Observable
- Timed

ASSIGNMENT FOR NEXT SESSION (1:10–1:15)

- Write a training objective
- Must be:
  1. Realistic to work environment
  2. Internet-related
  3. Complete (attainable in five minutes)

REVIEW (1:15–1:20)

SAMPLE SCRIPT

This sample script follows the lesson plan above. None of the scripts should be read verbatim; they are provided to give you ideas and a feel for how the lesson might go. Illustrated in this script are some general points to keep in mind:

- *Make the session very participatory; get them talking.*
- *Be enthusiastic; enthusiasm is infectious.*
- *Illustrate the points you are making about good training practices; be a good model.*

Introduction/Objectives (0:00–0:15)

Good morning! Welcome to the first session in our three-part "Internet Train the Trainers" series. I am really excited about this series, for a couple of reasons. One reason is that I think it is important to train our patrons on how to use the resources at the library, and especially on the Internet and other technologies, since it is so new to many of them. Personally, I love to do training sessions. A training workshop with a small group of patrons is a great way to spend some quality time with them and it can be really gratifying for us. And patrons are almost always incredibly grateful and appreciative.

The other reason I am excited about these workshops is that I know you are all experienced trainers. Many of you have already been conducting training sessions, or you have in the past. Or you have been teachers, or have conducted bibliographic instruction. And, in any case, each of you helps your patrons to use the Internet and the other resources at the library all the time; you train people every day. So I know that I am going to learn as much from you as you are going to learn from me. We are all going to learn from each other.

I know just about everybody, but for those of you I don't know yet, my name is [*your name*] and I work [*say where you work and what you do*].

What I'd like to do next is to take a couple of minutes and have you all pair off and introduce yourselves to a partner, and then introduce your partner to the rest of the group. I'd like you to focus on three things when you are talking to your partner and when you do your introductions:

[Write these on the board or a flip chart, as you say them.]

1. Who you are, where you work, and what you do. [*Write: Who, where, and what*]
2. What your experience is, if any, conducting Internet training for the public. [*Write: Experience?*]

3. What your objectives are for this "train the trainers" series. [*Write: Objectives?*] In other words, what would you like to get out of this?

OK, let's take about four minutes.

> [*Pair them up and give them four minutes. If you have an odd number of students, make one group a group of three.*]

OK! Well, I hate to break up these good conversations, but we should probably keep going. Why don't we start in the back there. Please introduce your partner and tell us about the three things we talked about.

> [*Have the participants introduce each other. As they introduce their objectives for the sessions, write them on the board or flip chart. Be very welcoming and thank them for the introductions.*]

Thank you. I am very glad to have everyone here. As I said, my name is [*your name*], and one of my main objectives is to meet your objectives in these training sessions. Here is what I heard:

> [*Review the objectives you have on the board. Typically, they will be things that you are going to cover in the session. Sometimes, however, they won't be, or they will be only partially related. For example, you might get, "I want to learn about more useful sites on the Internet," or "I want to learn more about search engines." Be honest and say that this is a series about good training techniques and practices. Also say something like: "While the focus of the training isn't on the Internet per se, we will be covering and presenting a lot of Internet topics, and in my experience I always learn something new about the Internet when I do one of these sessions. I'm sure that's going to be the case here." And it will be.*]

Here are some more objectives I came up with for this three-part series:

> [*Have the three objectives already written on the board or flip chart, and reveal them at this time.*]

At the end of this three-part series you should be able to

1. explain basic principles of learning;
2. apply those principles to the design of solid Internet training sessions for your patrons; and
3. conduct effective Internet training sessions with confidence.

Agenda For Three-Part Series: Review (0:15–0:20)

[Take five minutes to review logistical arrangements, objectives, and agenda.]

Review Packet (0:20–0:25)

[Take five minutes to review the contents of their training packets. The packet should include:

- *The handout for this series (see pages 34–44)*
- *A written agenda for the three-part "Internet Train the Trainers" series*
- *The model "Getting Started on the World Wide Web" workshop in Chapter 5*
- *Possibly a recent article of interest, such as one about effective use of search engines*
- *Name tags, if attendees do not know each other.]*

Sample Introduction to the World Wide Web: Discussion (0:25–0:30)

[Next, review the model "Getting Started on the World Wide Web" workshop (see Chapter 4). As mentioned, this should have been distributed to the participants ahead of time (a week or so before), and they should have been asked to read through it. Ask them for at least one thing they liked about the class, and at least one thing they might do differently, or something they might include that isn't there. Use direct questions (i.e., call on people) if no one volunteers. Write their suggestions on the board or flip chart. There should be a lot of discussion and participation; after all, there is no one way that an introduction to the Web should be taught.]

Training Overview (0:30–0:40)

OK, next I'd like to turn to what it is we're talking about when we talk about training. And there are three points about good training that I'd like you all to remember when you think about conducting training sessions for your patrons.

[Have these written down ahead of time on a flip chart or board.]

These are also in your packets [*pages 34–44*], so don't worry about writing them down:

1. Training should be viewed from the trainee's point of view.
2. Training should result in some observable change in the trainee's behavior.
3. The observable change should be controlled and determined by the trainer.

These points may seem obvious, but let's elaborate on them a little bit and see how they are related. First: *Training should be viewed from the trainee's point of view*. Often training, and teaching of any kind, is looked at from the trainer's (not the trainee's) point of view. The trainer or teacher is thought to be very knowledgeable, and he or she will impart that knowledge to the trainee. In a way, it's as though the trainer will inject the trainee with his or her knowledge. The model for this type of teaching is the lecture, and the measurement for success would be if the teacher got through the entire lecture and covered all the material.

But training is really more complicated than that. The trainer can be the most knowledgeable person in the world about the subject, but if he or she doesn't convey that knowledge to the trainee, the training is not successful. And, really, training is at least as much about the student discovering what he or she already knows as it is about learning more from someone else. So it's best to judge training from the trainee's point of view: What does the trainee know now that he or she didn't know before? What can the trainee do now that he or she couldn't before?

The second point, then, is related: *Training should result in some observable change in the trainee's behavior*. We are really dealing mostly with skills-based training when we talk about Internet and other technology training. Of course, there's knowledge and information involved, too, but what we really need to focus on is *doing*. What will our patrons be able to do after the training that they couldn't do before? Too much Internet training involves lecture and background information: Where did the Internet come from? How does it work technologically? That's all interesting, but it won't help our patrons use the Internet or find the information they need.

The other reason to focus on behavior is that you can see it, you can measure it. Can that trainee type in a Web address and go to a Web site? Can he or she click on the Home button? These are things we as trainers can see, and we can then judge how successful the training has been and where to repeat or place more emphasis.

Which brings us to the third point: *The observable change should be controlled and determined by the trainer*. We have talked about training being from the trainee's point of view, and resulting in changes to the trainee's behavior. But that doesn't mean that all control is given over to the trainee. Instead, you as the trainer determine what those changes in behavior will be.

You plan the lesson and set the objectives for the session, and you control the training session as it is happening.

Learning Principles (0:40–0:55)

OK, with those principles of training in mind, let's talk about how people actually learn. There have been lots of studies on adult learning principles, and there are a few general rules of thumb. We're going to cover five learning principles, and these are written in your packets. (This may be a review for some of you.) Here is what we know:

ACTION

Learning is not passive. Instead, most people learn by doing, by being actively involved in their training, by trial and error. Having said that, then, what are some ways you can make your training sessions more active, more participatory?

[Get responses and write them on the flip chart or board as you go. Elaborate on each point as it comes up. Here are common responses and ways to elaborate. If you don't get some of these, add them at the end and talk about them.]

Hands-on. Hands-on training is a great way to learn. People tend to learn best what they do on their own. So, if you are doing training in a computer lab, by all means have them work on the machines themselves. Even if you are demonstrating for a small group, use volunteers if you can to work the machine. What's the risk? Yes, it can really slow you up, and sometimes you'll have to make the call to speed things along. But usually the benefits far outweigh the disadvantages.

Questions. Absolutely, ask lots of questions. Get them talking. Now, there are different types of questions you can ask, and all are useful in certain situations. Let's talk about that.

You may have heard of *open* versus *closed* questions. Open questions ask for elaboration, expansion; they don't have a yes or no, right or wrong answer. *What is your experience with the Internet? Why would you want to use the Internet? What kinds of information are available on the Internet?* These are examples of open questions. They are good to use with a warmed-up group, to get more information, to get them talking.

By contrast, a closed question usually gets a yes or no answer, or a short answer that is either correct or incorrect. *Which is the Stop button? What does ".com" stand for? Can you find the library's hours from its home page?* Closed questions are good to reinforce a point, or to make sure that the trainees have understood and retained something.

In addition to open versus closed questions, there are also *direct* versus *overhead* questions. A direct question is directed at an individual: *Michael, have you used the Internet at the library before? Mary, can you name a search engine?* Direct questions are good when you have a passive, non-talkative group, when you want to warm them up and get them talking.

An overhead question, on the other hand, is not directed at a single person but is asked of the entire group: *Has anyone used the Internet at the library before? Can anyone tell me the name of a search engine?* Overhead questions are good when the group is warmed up and comfortable talking. If you get nowhere with an overhead question, you can always go back to using direct questions.

Finally, there are *relay* and *return* questions. A relay question is one where, when you get a question from someone, you relay it to the entire group: *That's a good question, Ann—does anyone know the answer to Ann's question? Interesting question, John—does anyone have any experience with that?* Relay questions are good when you want to keep the group talking. (They can also be good when you don't know the answer!)

Return questions are ones you return to the person asking: *That's an interesting question, Lisa—why do you ask that? Good question, Jim—what do you think the answer might be?* Return questions are good if you don't quite understand the question or want to know more about the situation before you answer. They are also good if you think the person really knows the answer or would like to give an opinion or talk about his or her experience a little bit.

Group Activities. Group activities can be a great way to make the training sessions more active. These can be especially good if you have a really large or passive group. Break the group into small teams and give them some assignment or task, such as finding answers on the Internet to a set of questions. You can turn something like that into a contest or game, like a scavenger hunt, which is especially good if you are working with young people. This is a really good way for people to learn from each other.

Outside Assignments or Research. An effective teaching method is to give the trainees something to work on between sessions of a training series, or before coming to the training session. For example, I gave you all the assignment of reading the model "Getting Started on the World Wide Web" class before coming here today. Outside assignments work best when you are going to be seeing the group of trainees more than once.

Presentations. Another potential activity is to have participants make presentations to the other trainees. We're going to be learning a lot about that later!

Movement. Movement is great for a training session. Make people stand up, change seats. If you're talking about the books and magazines about the

Internet that are available at the library, walk the group over to the shelves where they are. Movement gets the blood going and wakes people up.

Role Play. Role play is a time-honored training technique. Some people don't like it, but it can be fun and useful at times.

Directed Learning. If you show trainees a video, tell them three things to look for. If you give them something to read, ask them to write down two questions they have about it. If you are demonstrating something on the computer screen, give them two things to watch for as you perform a function. These kinds of directed learning activities will engage the participants in the learning process.

Audience Suggestions. Audience suggestions are a great way to get your audience interested in what you are demonstrating. For example, if you are going to demonstrate Yahoo, ask the audience if they have a suggestion for something to search.

Now, there is a danger in this, of course. The suggestion may not produce good results, for whatever reason: there may not be anything very good available on the Web for the suggested topic, or it may be too complicated a query to demonstrate quickly.

A couple suggestions: You can always direct the audience suggestions to guarantee success. For instance (back to the Yahoo example), let's say you are demonstrating the categories under Sports. Once you get down to basketball, for example, ask if anyone has a favorite team; most likely you'll find sites for this.

Also, you can use failure as a learning experience. If a search doesn't produce results, explain why—and perhaps use that opportunity to suggest other resources at the library. But don't leave it at failure: always make sure you have a successful search ready to demonstrate.

ASSOCIATION

The second principle of adult learning I want to talk about is that of association. People learn new things by relating them to what they already know. They fit them into already-formed conceptual frameworks.

Everyone already knows a lot. We as trainers should begin with what trainees already know; we should help them relate new information to what they already know. This process is especially important for computer and technology training.

One good way to help people create associations is to use analogies. I love to use analogies when conducting Internet training. What are some analogies you can use when explaining Internet concepts like a URL to your patrons?

[Get responses and write them on the flip chart or board as you go. Elaborate points as they come up. Here are common responses. If you don't get some of these, add them at the end. You'll probably get ones from the audience that you hadn't heard before, which is great.]

Analogies for a URL:

- Telephone number
- Postal address

Analogies for a subject index like Yahoo:

- Card catalog
- Shelves of books at the library
- Index to a book

(Book and library analogies can be especially successful. They relate doing research on the Internet to doing research using other resources.)

Analogies for the Internet:

- Spider's web
- Book with no index or page numbers
- Vanity press
- Television, with the mouse like the remote control (Just as parents want to provide guidance and rules for what their children may and may not watch on television, so should they also set rules about Internet usage.)

RESISTANCE

The third principle of learning that I want to talk about is that trainees often come to training sessions with some sort of resistance. Luckily, most of the people who will be coming to your training sessions will want to be there; they will have come voluntarily and want to learn. So that's a big one we don't have to worry about; there's nothing worse than trying to train a group of folks who don't want to be there at all!

Still, there may be some resistance among the patrons who come for Internet training. Where do you think this resistance would come from?

[Get from the participants: Fear—being afraid of the technology. If you don't get this answer, supply it.]

Fear is probably the biggest area of resistance you'll experience when you do technology training. Patrons may feel insecure or embarrassed about their lack of knowledge. They may feel that everyone knows about computers and the Internet except them. So, what are the more common fears?

- That everyone's online except for them.
- That they are falling behind.
- That they can't use the library anymore.
- That they'll break the machine if they do something wrong.

These are real fears, and the best way to combat them is to acknowledge them. Bring them out in the open; ask questions about them. Acknowledge the resistance and establish a safe environment. Be encouraging. One of the best ways to make people feel more at ease is to tell a personal story. If it feels comfortable and real, tell them about your own experience learning about computers and the Internet, about how you may have overcome trepidation yourself.

SIMPLICITY

This is the fourth principle of adult learning. Keep it simple. Typically, we can only concentrate on one thing at a time, one concept at a time. Don't crowd the training agenda with "nice-to-know" information; focus instead on "need-to-know" information. This is especially important with technology and Internet training, where much of the information is new and can easily become overwhelming. Pare it down to the basics.

VARIETY

The last principle involves the importance of variety. Don't exceed 15 minutes of lecturing. Break up mini-lectures with activities and interaction.

Also, people learn differently, through different senses. Some people like to hear; some people like to do; some people like to read; some people like to say. Appeal to all the senses when you do training. That way, you're more likely to appeal to the different ways your audience learns. It's also a good way to reinforce points.

So we have covered five major principles of adult learning:

- Action
- Association
- Resistance
- Simplicity
- Variety

Last, let's turn to training objectives.

Training Objectives (0:55–1:10)

The last thing we're going to cover today is writing training objectives. The best way to get things done is to have goals, to work toward objectives. This method is also true in training, where writing good training objectives is the key to effective training.

I would like everyone to remember four things about good training objectives.

[Have these written down ahead of time on a flip chart or board.]

These are also in your packets, so don't worry about writing them down. Training objectives should be: specific, attainable, observable, and timed. Let's take those one at a time.

Good training objectives are very specific—as specific as possible. "Trainees will learn about the Internet" is not a good training objective. "Trainees will be able to type in a URL and connect to a site" is a fine training objective.

In addition, make your training objectives attainable. It's not realistic for folks who have never used the Internet to become expert searchers in an hour. It is more realistic that they will be able to use the mouse to scroll up and down and click on hyperlinks. There is a tendency to try to do too much, to expect too much too quickly; try to avoid that.

Focus on observable behavior. We have already talked about this a little bit. If you can't see that students can do something, it's harder to know whether they have learned or retained anything. Write your training objectives so that they focus on measurable, observable behaviors. This will also help you to focus on the trainee, rather than the trainer.

Finally, make your training objectives timed. They should have timed deadlines. "At the end of five minutes, trainees will be able to scroll up and down the screen." "At the end of ten minutes trainees will be able to get to Yahoo and perform a search." Timed objectives allow you to stick to the agenda, and to make adjustments if necessary. You should structure your entire lesson plan or agenda around these timed objectives. And they shouldn't be too long. Try for 5-, 10-, or 15-minute chunks; objectives that will take longer than that to accomplish should be broken down into smaller, discrete objectives.

Assignment for Next Session (1:10–1:15)

Your assignment for the next session is simple: to write one training objective. But remember: make it specific, attainable, observable, and timed. I am going to give you the time: five minutes. This should be a training objective that you can accomplish realistically in five minutes. Now, five minutes is not a lot of time, so make it very specific and targeted. But I want you to make it complete: something that can truly be completed and accomplished in five minutes. I also want it to be realistic to your work environment and your patrons. Make your training objective something that you can realistically imagine yourself using with your patrons in an Internet training session.

So that won't be so hard! And I am going to make it even easier; I am going to give you a model for writing your objective, which you can use or adapt as you wish:

"After five minutes, the trainees will be able to . . . "

For example, "After five minutes, trainees will be able to make a ham and cheese sandwich." But, of course, yours has to be something Internet-related!

OK? You don't have to outline how you'd accomplish the objective—we'll get to that later. But perhaps start thinking about the methods you would use. Any questions?

Review (1:15–1:20)

OK, let's just quickly recap what we covered today.

We reviewed the sample "Getting Started on the World Wide Web" workshop–both its strengths, and some of the things that could be done differently.

We talked about what training is, and that:

1. Training should be viewed from the trainee's point of view.
2. Training should result in some observable change in the trainee's behavior.
3. The observable change should be controlled and determined by the trainer.

We went over five adult learning principles—how people learn—and how to apply those principles to our training sessions:

- Action: Make your sessions active through questions and activities.
- Association: Help people create associations from new things to things they already know; use analogies for foreign concepts.
- Resistance: People tend to have resistance of some kind; probably the major one we'll encounter is fear of technology.
- Simplicity: Focus on "need-to-know" information only.
- Variety: Appeal to different senses and learning styles.

Finally, we just talked about training objectives, and how they are the key to effective training. Good training objectives are:

- Specific
- Attainable
- Observable
- Timed

That's it for today. Please bring your packet back with you to the next session, along with your five-minute training objective. See you next time!

Chapter 2
Internet Train
the Trainers
(Part 2)

> **Handouts for this workshop follow page 33.**

OVERVIEW

Who

This is Part 2 of the three-part "Internet Train the Trainers" series. Ideally, the audience for this workshop is the same group of people who attended Part 1 together. It is important that the group build trust and rapport; they will feel more comfortable taking risks, making mistakes, and giving honest assessments of the presentations of the others. It will also help create a committed "team" of trainers. However, even if the participants did not take Part 1 together, they will all need to have taken it before taking Part 2. It should be required that participants complete the three parts of the series in sequence.

What

Part 2 of this series focuses on presentation skills, content structure, and group dynamics. It also reviews Part 1 and lays the groundwork for Part 3.

Where

Like Part 1, this workshop is designed for a computer lab with space for ten students and the instructor (11 computers with Internet access, one with projection for the instructor). This computer lab is also used for public training sessions; some of the students will conduct their Internet training sessions here. However, this workshop could easily be adapted to another setting (such as a larger lab, a lecture hall, or a room with one computer); in fact, it is not necessary that this session or Part 1 take place in the computer lab. This series is designed to be adaptable so that students can apply what they learn to whatever training setting is realistic for them.

When

This session should be offered fairly soon after Part 1, but allowing attendees enough time to complete the assignment from Part 1. A week or less is ideal.

This session lasts an hour and 10 minutes.

Why

The objectives of this three-part series are for the trainees to be able to (1) explain basic principles of learning; (2) apply those principles to the design of solid Internet training sessions for their patrons; and (3) conduct effective Internet training sessions with confidence.

The objectives for Part 2 are for the trainees to be able to (1) incorporate solid, content-related presentation skills into their training sessions; (2) replicate effective, style-related presentation skills; and (3) manage with confidence the unexpected difficulties that may occur in training sessions.

WORKSHOP AGENDA

Again, this agenda is crowded, so it is important to maintain control. At the same time, you want to encourage participants to talk and to share their knowledge and experience. Be encouraging and empathetic; you want to build their confidence as trainers. You also want to make them understand that everyone encounters difficult experiences in training and that they can handle these situations because they will be fully prepared.

REVIEW/OBJECTIVES (0:00–0:10) *Outline*

- Quick review of last session
- Objectives for this session—Trainees will be able to:
  1. Incorporate solid, content-related presentation skills into training sessions
  2. Replicate effective, style-related presentation skills
  3. Manage with confidence the unexpected difficulties that occur in training sessions

TRAINING OBJECTIVES ASSIGNMENT: REVIEW (0:10–0:20)

PRESENTATION SKILLS (0:20–0:40)

- Content: action, association, simplicity, variety, clear objective—plus:
  1. Repetition
  2. Three-part structure
  3. Primacy and recentness
  4. Appropriateness
  5. Examples
  6. Control of time
  7. Leadership
- Presentation: you want to convey authority, enthusiasm, responsiveness:
  1. Smile
  2. Make eye contact
  3. Relax your shoulders
  4. Don't read
  5. Place notes in convenient location
  6. Stand
  7. Move
  8. Don't turn your back on the audience
  9. Slow down

NIGHTMARES IN TRAINING, OR MURPHY'S LAW (0:40–0:55)

- Questions you can't answer
- Irrelevant questions
- Passive groups
- Disruptive groups
- Know-it-alls
- Equipment failure

ASSIGNMENT FOR NEXT SESSION (0:55–1:05)

- Five-minute practice presentations
- Any audience, setting
- Can use the objective written for this session, or a new one, but it must be:
    1. Realistic to work environment
    2. Internet-related
    3. Complete (attainable in five minutes)

REVIEW (1:05–1:10)

SAMPLE SCRIPT

This sample script follows the lesson plan above. Once again, do not not read it verbatim but use it for ideas. Illustrated in this script are some general points to keep in mind:

- *Make the session very participatory; get them talking.*
- *Be encouraging; empathize with their "nightmares" in training.*
- *Illustrate the points you are making about good training practices; be a good model.*

Review/Objectives (0:00–0:10)

Welcome back! This is Part 2 of our "Internet Train the Trainers" series. It's great to see everyone again.

As you recall, in Part 1 we reviewed the sample "Introduction to the World Wide Web" workshop—both its strengths, and some of the things that could be done differently.

We also talked about what training is, and some important considerations:

1. Training should be viewed from the trainee's (not the trainer's) point of view;
2. Training should result in some observable change in the trainee's behavior; and
3. The observable change should be controlled and determined by the trainer.

We went over five learning principles—how people learn—and how to apply those principles to our training sessions:

- Action: Make your sessions active through questions and activities.
- Association: Help people create associations from new things to things they already know; use analogies for foreign concepts.
- Resistance: People tend to have resistance of some kind; probably the major one we'll encounter is fear of technology.
- Simplicity: Focus on "need-to-know" information only.
- Variety: Appeal to different senses and learning styles.

And finally, we talked about training objectives, and how they are the key to effective training. Good training objectives are:

- Specific
- Attainable
- Observable
- Timed

The objectives for this session are for you to be able to:

1. Incorporate solid, content-related presentation skills into training sessions
2. Replicate effective, style-related presentation skills
3. Manage with confidence the unexpected difficulties that occur in training sessions.

Training Objectives Assignment: Review (0:10–0:20)

OK, we just talked about some of the characteristics of good training objectives: specific, attainable, observable, and timed. You all had an assignment from last time to write an Internet training objective that could be accomplished in five minutes. Let's hear some of them! Who wants to go first?

[If no one volunteers to go first, call on someone. If you only have ten or so people in the training session, go through everyone's objective. Have each person read the objective, and then discuss each one with the group. One of the most common "problems" will be that the goal will be too big to accomplish realistically in five minutes. In addition, some of the objectives may not be specific enough. As you discuss each objective, ask the entire group for feedback, and for ideas on how it could be improved, if necessary. Be encouraging of everyone's efforts, and make sure a positive, workable objective emerges for everyone.]

Presentation Skills (0:20–0:40)

OK, thanks everyone. Those objectives are great, and we'll turn back to those again at the end of today's session.

What I'd like to talk about next is good presentation skills, both in terms of content and also in terms of presentation style.

We've all sat through presentations and speeches that were deadly. They drone on and on, and you think it's never going to end. Some speakers are so fidgety they make you nervous just watching them. Or they look like they can't wait until it's over. The speaker may be the most knowledgeable person in the world, but if he or she can't present well, the audience isn't going to get anything out of it, or won't get as much as they should.

CONTENT

First let's talk about content: how to structure it, how to control it. We've already talked about how people learn—about how you want to incorporate action, association, simplicity, variety, and clear objectives into your training. Let's build on that.

[Write each point on the board or flip chart as you talk about it.]

I've just illustrated one important element of presenting your content: *repetition*. In training, you want to repeat, repeat, repeat. Say important points more than once; then it will stick. I know I often need to hear things more than once to have them sink in; emphasize the important points by repeating them. Redundancy is a good thing in training.

This also leads into the next content presentation element, one that is a cardinal rule of presentations and one that you may have already heard about. And that is the classic *three-part structure*, which goes like this:

First, introduce the presentation or workshop: tell them what you are going to tell them. State the objectives or the three main points of the session.

Next, tell them. This is the main portion of the session. You will probably want to break this portion down into three main sections or topics.

Finally, when you're done, finish the session by telling them what you told them. Recap the session by repeating the three main points you want them to remember.

This structure has the benefit of repetition and simplicity. It also works because it follows two other rules: *primacy* and *recentness*. In general, most people remember the first things they hear and the most recent things they have heard. Everything else—everything in the middle—is more up in the air; some people will remember certain things, others will remember other things.

If you repeat the most important three points at the beginning and at the end, it's more likely that everybody will at least remember those.

Always make your training *appropriate* to the audience. For example, if your audience consists of senior citizens, you may have to spend more time showing basic computer skills, though this is a generalization, of course. If they are teenagers, you probably won't need to do that, and can go right to the sites themselves. Always target your training to your audience's knowledge, experience, and abilities. And, in all cases, avoid jargon as much as possible, and don't assume that technical terms that may seem obvious are, in fact, common knowledge. If you must use jargon, provide definitions.

Use *examples* that are grounded in reality. People learn what they need to know, what is relevant to their situations. If they don't need to know something, there is little reason for them to remember it. So, if you're demonstrating what is useful and fun about the Internet, choose examples that you think your audience will be interested in. Again, you have to know your audience, your patrons. Are they teenagers or adults? Seniors? What are their backgrounds?

What are some topics, subjects, or Web sites that you think your audience members would be interested in and that would be good to demonstrate on the Internet?

[*Get responses and talk about them individually. Ask your trainees why they like to use those sites or topics. Have some examples that you like to use, as well. For instance, I like to demonstrate job information sites such as Careerpath.com; news sites such as CNN, MSNBC, or USA Today; and telephone directories on the Web. These are things that most adults are interested in—everyone wants to look up an old college roommate or an ex-boyfriend or ex-girlfriend, for instance. They are good, all-purpose sites and topics.*]

Maintain *control of time*. Stick to the agenda and have time markers throughout the outline or lesson plan. This is not always so easy. Everything takes longer than expected, especially the first time you conduct a session. When you practice alone, you don't have questions, you aren't using volunteers, and you may not actually be performing the searches. When it comes to the actual session, things can easily take twice as long as you think they will. Always wear a watch, or make sure the clock works where you will be doing the training.

Finally, be a good *leader*. You, as the trainer, are the only one who can maintain control of the time, the agenda, the objectives. And nearly everyone in your audience will want to see you succeed in doing that. In addition to adhering to the agenda and the objectives, good leadership skills include:

- Listening to questions, clarifying, and responding
- Protecting everyone's rights
- Questioning silent participants, drawing them in
- Recapping main points
- Being prepared
- Showing enthusiasm

PRESENTATION

Now let's turn to actual presentation skills, or style of presentation. We have all seen bad presenters. What are some of the things bad presenters do?

[Get responses. Talk about them. Use yourself to demonstrate bad and good presentation skills.]

Now let's talk about some good presentation skills. The three most important things you want to convey to your audience are authority, enthusiasm, and responsiveness to the participants. In order to convey these three things, here are some tips:

[Use yourself to demonstrate.]

Smile. This seems simple and obvious, but it's not something people do very often or very easily when giving presentations. It is something that you have to train yourself to do, and it may feel awkward at first. But it works. People feel good when you smile at them, they smile back at you, and everyone relaxes and feels better.

Make eye contact. Again, this can be tough to do, and you will have to practice. You will feel self-conscious at first, but after a while it will start to feel natural. What you want to do is make sustained eye contact with every single person in the audience (as long as we're not talking about a big lecture hall with hundreds of people.) Look at one person, make eye contact, talk directly to that person for five to ten seconds, then move on to another person. Don't dart around too quickly, and don't focus on any one person for too long—they might start to feel uncomfortable! But if you actually look at everybody in the room, then everybody will feel involved in the program.

Relax your shoulders. When they are giving presentations, people tend to tense up their shoulders. Don't slump, but let your shoulders relax. Your whole body will relax, and you'll feel much better.

Don't read. There is nothing worse than listening to a presenter who is reading verbatim from a prepared speech. Never read. Work from an outline with bulleted points—not complete sentences. You'll maintain a more conversational tone that way, and you'll look up at the audience more.

Place notes in a convenient location. Try not to hold anything (including notes) in your hands. Put your notes down on a table, if possible—somewhere you can walk by naturally when you need to glance down at them. If you must hold notes, use small note cards instead of big, floppy pieces of paper.

Stand. Standing is more authoritative than sitting down and allows you to move around. It also usually makes it easier for your audience to see you. If you must sit, or if you really prefer it, pick an authoritative position—for example, perched on a desk, above your audience. Try to avoid standing or sitting behind anything, such as a lectern or a desk. Move out from behind it, and toward your audience.

Move. Movement is good, but don't run around constantly. Move, and then take a stand, with your feet firmly planted. Don't rock back and forth, cross your feet, or lean on one foot. When you move, move into your audience, not away from them.

Don't turn your back on the audience. This can actually be a tough one, especially when you're demonstrating something on a computer. But don't talk to the machine; talk to the audience. Do what you need to do on the computer, and then turn back to your audience. Also, if you are using an overhead, don't talk to the projection screen or wall. Make sure the slide or projection looks OK on the screen, and then turn and talk to the audience.

Slow down. When people get nervous, they tend to talk faster. But your audience needs time to process what you're saying. Come to full stops at the end of sentences. Breathe.

Nightmares in Training, or Murphy's Law (0:40–0:55)

OK, now that we've talked about the good stuff, let's talk about the bad stuff: nightmares in training.

It's Murphy's Law: if something can possibly go wrong, it will, and at the most inopportune moment. Something is bound to go wrong when you are doing training. Maybe not the first time; maybe not the first few times. But, trust me, some time, when you least expect it, it will.

The key is to be confident, and the way to be confident is to be prepared. And you will all be prepared.

What are some potential nightmares in training—things that have gone wrong for you in the past, or that you imagine could go wrong in the future?

> [Get responses. Write them on the flip chart or board, and talk about each of them as they come up. If any of the following aren't mentioned, talk about them at the end.]

Questions you can't answer. None of us knows everything, and as technology trainers, we'll get asked all sorts of questions we may not be able to answer, and shouldn't be expected to answer. Everything from "What kind of computer should I buy?" to an arcane question about a piece of software we may have never used.

The first rule when this happens is: Don't try to hide it. Don't try to cover up the fact that you don't know the answer. Usually, this will backfire. It will be obvious that you don't know.

Instead, acknowledge that you don't know the answer. Say something like, "That's a good question. I don't have the answer for that one." Then you have a number of options, depending on the question and the group:

- You can relay the question to the whole group. This works if you have time in the agenda, if you think the question is of widespread interest to the group, and if you feel confident that someone in the group may know the answer.
- You can offer to do some research later and get back to them, either in person, by phone, or by e-mail. Usually you'll want to offer to meet with the person for a few minutes after the session. This can work if you feel you would like to know the answer to the question, or perhaps should know the answer. It also works well with repeat customers whom you are sure to see again.
- You can offer to refer the person asking the question to sources of information where the answer may be found. Again you can offer to meet with the person for a few minutes after the session. This is a good tactic if the question is fairly obscure or particular to that person's situation, and may take some time to research. This is a perfectly valid response; referring patrons to sources of information is, after all, something that we do every day.

Irrelevant and obscure questions. People ask all kinds of questions during a workshop, many of them not related to the topic at hand or only obscurely relevant, others very particular to a participant's concerns and interests. Don't take up the entire group's time answering these types of questions; it's important to respect their rights by staying on topic. On the other hand, it is also important to respond to the participant posing the question.

The best approach is to acknowledge the question, offer to speak with the person who asked the question after the session, restate the objective you are working on, and move on. Say something like, "That's an excellent question. Unfortunately, we don't have time in this session to cover that, but let's talk for a few minutes after class about this, OK? Great. So, we were discussing the various types of search engines . . . "

Remember, you are in control of the agenda.

Passive groups. Some groups are like statues: they won't talk, they won't participate, they won't laugh, nothing. What do you do with a group like that?

Well, first try a few tactics to bring them out. The most effective one is to ask direct questions. Pick someone in the group who looks willing to talk, and ask him or her a direct, nonthreatening question. Try this tactic with a few people; eventually, the group may warm up.

Have some of the activities we talked about in the last session ready to use when necessary. For example, have a group activity ready to go, where people have to work in pairs. Or ask them to identify three kinds of links on a Web page. Nothing too threatening.

If everything fails, give up and lecture. Lecturing can be useful; they'll still learn a lot.

Disruptive groups. Sometimes two or three people will develop a side conversation, and even if it is about the topic of the training, it can be disruptive to you and to the rest of the group.

In group dynamics, everybody knows what is going on at all times. When someone is being disruptive, everyone in the group knows it and feels it; you can't just ignore the situation. As we discussed earlier, the trainer is the leader of the group, and only the leader can take care of the problem of a disruptive person or side group. Everyone expects the leader to take care of the problem, and the group's sympathies are almost always with the leader in this kind of situation.

Teachers know that one way to take care of the problem is ask if the disruptive ones have a question, or something they would like to share. Another very effective method is simply to stand near them. Walk over to where they are and lecture from there. Believe me, they'll quickly stop talking. If these techniques don't work, stop talking and stare at them until they realize they are being a problem. You can also ask them to be quiet. And if all else fails, insist that they leave.

Know-it-alls. Often someone in the group will try to dominate. He or she will answer every question you ask; will ask lots of obscure questions; will offer information that is too technical for the topic and the group. Typically, such folks are trying to show that they are knowledgeable. Sometimes they are, and sometimes they aren't.

Here are a couple of rules when dealing with these folks. First, don't try to win. Even if you disagree with their points, don't get into a confrontation or a debate. They are unlikely to back down. Second, don't put down the know-it-all. Even though it's your responsibility to take control of the situation and steer the session back to the agenda, you need to do this in a respectful way. Aside from being the decent thing to do, you'll also keep the respect and sympathies of the rest of the group.

The best thing to do is to smile, thank him or her for their contribution, and move on. If you are asked a question that is only tangentially relevant, say "That's a very interesting question. Unfortunately, we don't have time to cover that now, but let's talk about this after class. OK? Thanks." If a know-it-all is the only one volunteering to answer questions, just don't call on him or her, or say nicely "Let's hear from someone else this time," and call on someone else.

Equipment failure. This is usually the primary disaster that technology trainers worry about, but it really shouldn't be. Yes, it's bound to happen sooner or later. The server goes down, the instructor's computer crashes—something. The key is to be prepared.

You can always lecture, and you should always have a nontechnical backup. For example, if you can, have an overhead projector for transparencies, and have some transparencies ready to go. For example, if one item on your lesson plan is to talk about Yahoo, you should have a transparency slide of the home page of Yahoo. You can easily use that slide as you talk about Yahoo's features and potential uses.

Another backup measure is to have files loaded locally to your hard drive. That way, if your network connection is down, you can still bring up sample Web pages. To take our Yahoo example again, you can save on your hard drive (or on a floppy that you carry with you) an HTML file of Yahoo's home page. You can do this in your browser by going under File/Save As, and saving the file.

[Demonstrate this, so that everyone knows.]

Then, if your connection is down, bring up Yahoo's page locally. In your browser, choose File/Open, and choose the file on your hard drive or your floppy.

[Demonstrate this, so that everyone knows.]

Don't worry too much about equipment failure. If your computers fail, try to fix the problem. But if you can't fix it quickly, move on; don't spend the entire training session trying to troubleshoot. Keep a positive, upbeat attitude, shrug it off, haul out your transparencies and lecture notes, and go from there. While the participants may lose their hands-on opportunities, equipment failure can, in fact, also be an opportunity. It allows more time for lecture and questions. Your training session can still be a great session.

Assignment for Next Session (0:55–1:05)

Let's talk about the next session, which is the third and final session of our "Internet Train the Trainers" series. We have talked about how people learn best by doing, so we are going to put that principle into practice!

Next time, each of you will give a practice five-minute training session to the rest of us. We want this to be as realistic as possible, so here's how we're going to do it.

We will be your audience, your students. But we can be anyone you want us to be—we'll act the parts. We can be a group of kids who have come with a class, we can be senior citizens, the general public who signed up for an Introduction to the Internet . . . anything. You will just need to tell as at the beginning who we are. And I want you to pick an audience that is realistic for you in your work environment, a group that you can imagine yourself actually training in your work setting.

Similarly, the setting can be anything you want it to be, as long as it is realistic for you. So if you will be doing your training in this computer lab or some other computer lab, by all means use the machines and make it a hands-on training. If you will be conducting your training gathered around one machine, we'll all gather around the machine up at the front. If you will be lecturing, we can be your audience. But please make it as realistic a setting as possible, one that is as similar as possible to your actual training setting.

All of the materials will be here: the computers, the computer projection, the overhead for transparencies, the flip chart. Feel free to use whatever you need.

I want each of you to have a training objective that is realistic for your audience and attainable in five minutes. You can use the objective you wrote for your assignment last time, modify it, or have a completely new one. It's up to you. The only requirements are that it be realistic to your work environment, that it be Internet-related, and that it be a *complete* objective—attainable in five minutes. In addition to telling us who we are, at the beginning of your presentation you should also tell us what your objective is.

And we're going to be strict about the five-minute rule, which is not a lot of time; otherwise, we won't get through everyone. After each of you gives your presentation, we will all give you feedback, both on content and on presentation style. Things that went well, and things to watch out for or maybe to do a little differently in the future.

This will be fun—I promise! And, remember, this is just practice, so feel free to experiment. Maybe try some things out that you haven't tried before. Take a few risks, if you want. This is the place to do it. And remember all the good things we have talked about in these two sessions so far. Make it active and participatory, smile, make eye contact—all those good things.

Are there any questions?

I am going to put out a sheet for you to sign on your way out, to determine the order you go in. Some people like to go at the beginning, others like to wait. This is your chance!

Review (1:05–1:10)

Let's review what we went over today.

We went through your great training objectives, and made them as specific, attainable, and observable as possible, and we also made sure they could be accomplished in the allotted time frame.

Next we turned to presentation skills, and talked about how both content and presentation style are very important when conducting training.

In terms of content, some of the key points to remember are: repetition of the most important elements; the classic three-part structure of presentations; primacy and recentness; appropriateness; the use of examples based in reality; and maintaining control of time and showing good leadership skills.

In terms of presentation style, remember always to smile; make eye contact with everyone in the room; face your audience and move into them; don't stand or sit behind anything; don't read; and talk slowly.

Finally, we just talked about nightmares in the classroom and how to handle them. The key is to be prepared, and to have backups.

Thanks for coming! See you next time for our presentations! Don't forget to sign up on your way out.

3
Internet Train the Trainers (Part 3)

> **Handouts for this workshop follow page 33.**

OVERVIEW

Who

This is Part 3 of the three-part "Internet Train the Trainers" series. Ideally, the audience for this workshop is the same group of people who attended Parts 1 and 2 together; this helps to build trust and a committed "team" of trainers. However, even if the participants did not take Parts 1 and 2 together, they will all need to have taken them, in sequence, before taking Part 3.

What

Part 3 of this series consists entirely of practice presentations and critiques. It puts into practice what has been learned in the first two sessions.

Where

This session should take place in the same computer lab as Parts 1 and 2. This computer lab, with space for ten students and the instructor, is also used for public training sessions; some of the students will conduct their real Internet training sessions here.

When

This session should be offered fairly soon after Part 2, but allowing attendees enough time to complete the assignment. One week is ideal.

This session lasts for two-and-a-half hours.

Why

The objectives of this three-part series are for the trainees to be able to (1) explain basic principles of learning; (2) apply those principles to the design of solid Internet training sessions for their patrons; and (3) conduct effective Internet training sessions with confidence.

The objectives for Part 3 are for the trainees to be able to (1) design a sound training module around a clear objective; (2) conduct an effective training session with confidence; and (3) recognize strengths and weaknesses in the training practices of others and incorporate that knowledge into their own training.

PROCEDURE

This session will consist entirely of practice presentations. To a great extent, it will take care of itself and will be the highlight of the "Internet Train the Trainers" series.

If there are ten presenters, the session should last about two-and-a-half hours. That will give each presentation a little less than 15 minutes total, which will include setup, introductions, the presentation itself, and critiques. The actual presentations should last five minutes each, and you will need to be fairly strict about that. Take a ten-minute break in the middle, after half of the presenters have finished.

Begin the session by welcoming everyone back and reviewing what should happen.

Hand out the order of presentations. This sheet should have two columns. The first column should have the names of the presenters in order; the second column should have the names of the first reactors in order. (Type up the list of presenters in the order they signed up following Part 2; supply the reactors yourself, and make sure that everyone is a reactor once.)

Ask for a volunteer timekeeper. Have signs prepared for that person to hold up at "One Minute to Go" and "Done," and instruct the participants that they will really need to wrap it up when the "Done" sign goes up, if they haven't already. You might want to have two volunteer timekeepers—one for the first five presenters, and one for the second.

Remind the presenters to set the scene at the beginning: to tell the class who the audience is ("tell us who we are") and to tell them if they want the audience to remain seated, to gather around the machine at the front, and so on. Volunteer to help set up, pass out handouts, or do whatever else is needed at the beginning.

Remind them to state the objective of the lesson at the beginning of their presentation. Remind them to think about things that were covered in the first two sessions: to smile, to make eye contact, but most of all to enjoy it.

After each person gives his or her presentation, have that person remain in front of the group and ask the first reactor for that presenter to give feedback, focusing on content and presentation skills: what worked well, what could have been done differently. Then ask for reactions of the others, and give your reactions as well. Be very positive and encouraging for everyone, but don't hesitate to point out specific areas for improvement. A round of applause for each presenter after the feedback has been given is always nice.

You may want to write out a sheet of notes for each presenter and give it to him or her afterwards. Again, be positive and encouraging, and point out specific areas for improvement.

One option for this session is to videotape each presenter and give each his or her own tape to take home. This practice can do wonders; it can really add visual reinforcement to the verbal feedback. If you decide to do this and have access to the equipment, ask for a volunteer in the group to operate the camera, or have an assistant do it.

Close the session by thanking everyone. Ask for questions and final thoughts about what they learned from the experience today. Review any logistical details about the training program in the library system, and cover support that they can expect to receive (such as copies of handouts, publicity, staff resources). Remind them that the handouts cover all the major points in the sessions. Encourage them to put what they have learned into practice as soon as possible. Be inspiring and encouraging!

INTERNET TRAIN THE TRAINERS (PART 1) AGENDA

Introduction/Objectives
- Welcome and introductions
- Participants' objectives for three-part series
- Trainer's objectives for three-part series
    1. Explain principles of learning
    2. Apply those principles to the design of solid Internet training sessions
    3. Conduct effective Internet training sessions with confidence.

Agenda for the Three-Part Series: Review

Review Packet

Sample Introduction to the World Wide Web: Discussion
- Strengths
- What could be done differently

Training Overview
- From trainee's point of view
- Measurable, observable, behavioral change
- Controlled by trainer

Learning Principles
- Action
- Association
- Resistance
- Simplicity
- Variety

Training Objectives
- Specific
- Attainable
- Observable
- Timed

Assignment for Next Session
- Writing a training objective
- Must be:
    1. Realistic to work environment
    2. Internet-related
    3. Complete (attainable in five minutes)

INTERNET TRAIN THE TRAINERS (PART 2) AGENDA

Review/Objectives
- Quick review of last session
- Objectives for this session—Trainees will be able to:
    1. Incorporate solid, content-related presentation skills into training sessions
    2. Replicate effective, style-related presentation skills
    3. Manage with confidence the unexpected difficulties that occur in training sessions.

Training Objectives Assignment: Review

Presentation Skills
- Content: action, association, simplicity, variety, clear objective—plus:
    1. Repetition
    2. Three-part structure
    3. Primacy and recentness
    4. Appropriateness
    5. Examples
    6. Control of time
    7. Leadership
- Presentation: you want to convey authority, enthusiasm, responsiveness:
    1. Smile
    2. Make eye contact
    3. Relax your shoulders
    4. Don't read
    5. Place notes in convenient location
    6. Stand
    7. Move
    8. Don't turn your back on the audience
    9. Slow down

Nightmares in Training, or Murphy's Law
- Questions
- Irrelevant questions
- Passive groups
- Disruptive groups
- Know-it-alls
- Equipment failure

Assignment for Next Session
- Five-minute practice presentations

INTERNET TRAIN THE TRAINERS (PART 2) AGENDA—(CONTINUED)

- Any audience, setting
- Can use the objective written for this session, or a new one, but it must be:
  1. Realistic to work environment
  2. Internet-related
  3. Complete (attainable in five minutes)

INTERNET TRAIN THE TRAINERS (PART 3) AGENDA

Presentation of Practice Training Sessions
- Presentation
- Reaction
  Repeat until all participants have done a presentation and a reaction.

INTERNET TRAIN THE TRAINERS

KEY TRAINING POINTS

Training Overview

- *From trainee's point of view.* Think of training from the trainee's (not the trainer's) point of view.
- *Measurable, observable, behavioral change.* Training should result in some measurable, observable change in the trainee's actions. What can the trainee do now that he or she could not do before?
- *Controlled by trainer.* The trainer is the leader. The trainer determines the objectives for the training session, and makes sure that those objectives are met.

Learning Principles

- *Action.* Most people learn best by doing, by trial and error. Make your sessions as active as you can. As much as possible, have attendees perform tasks themselves, rather than observing. Insert activity and dialog into your sessions by using questions, games, activities, outside assignments, and directed learning.
- *Association.* Most people learn by associating new information to what they already know. Help trainees to discover and make these associations by using analogies to known information and common activities.
- *Resistance.* Many participants will feel some sort of resistance in any given training session. For technology training in a library setting, the most common form of resistance will be fear. As a trainer, bring those fears out into the open, acknowledge them, and invite participants to discuss them. Be reassuring and encouraging.
- *Simplicity.* Most training workshops try to pack too much information into one session. Keep it simple. Stick to "need-to-know" information only.
- *Variety.* Everyone learns differently. Try to appeal to as many senses as possible (such as touch, sight, hearing). Use a variety of techniques (including lecture, demonstration, hands-on, handouts) to reinforce information.

Training Objectives

- *Specific.* Make your training objectives as specific as possible. Target them to small actions that can be accomplished. Break large concepts into specific, discrete objectives.
- *Attainable.* Make your objectives realistic. Know your audience's knowledge and experience, and target your objectives appropriately.
- *Observable.* When writing your training objectives, focus on observable actions. Tie them to skills that you can see, allowing you to evaluate easily whether trainees have mastered the activity and met the objectives.

- *Timed.* Allow a specific amount of time for each objective, and structure your lesson plan or agenda around these timed objectives. Short time frames (5, 10, or 15 minutes) are the most effective.

Presentation Skills

Content—action, association, simplicity, variety, clear objective—plus:
- *Repetition.* Repeat important information. Reinforce key points in different ways: handouts, flip charts, overheads, and different vocabulary.
- *Three-part structure.* Tell them what you are going to tell them. Tell them. Tell them what you told them.
- *Primacy and recentness.* People remember best what they hear first and what they have just heard. Use these sessions wisely to introduce and reinforce the most important points.
- *Appropriateness.* Make your training session appropriate to your audience. Target the content and the speed to their experience, knowledge, and abilities.
- *Examples.* Use examples from real life to ground concepts in reality. Involve your audience by asking them for examples. Choose examples that are important to your trainees.
- *Control of time.* As the leader, you must maintain control of time, keep to the agenda, and ensure that objectives are met. Have time markers throughout your lesson plan. Wear a watch. Plan time wisely: in a real training setting, things almost always take longer than expected.
- *Leadership.* Demonstrate good leadership skills, including adhering to the agenda; listening to questions and responding; protecting everyone's rights; summarizing main points; drawing in silent participants; showing enthusiasm; being prepared.

Presentation—you want to convey authority, enthusiasm, responsiveness:
- *Smile.* It may feel unnatural at first to smile during a presentation, but it will feel more natural after you practice. Smiling makes everyone (including yourself) feel more relaxed.
- *Make eye contact.* Make sustained eye contact with members of your audience—with every single person, if it is a small enough group. Talk directly to individuals, not over their heads. Again, this will feel more natural after you practice.
- *Relax your shoulders.* This will help your whole body to relax. Pay attention to your shoulders at various points throughout the session.
- *Don't read.* Never read notes verbatim. Have bulleted talking points, not full sentences, written down. Index cards, rather than sheets of paper, work well.
- *Place notes in a convenient location.* Try not to hold anything (including notes) in your hands. Instead, place your note cards where you can walk by them naturally.
- *Stand.* Usually, it is best to stand. If you sit, try to sit above your audience so that you are in an authoritative position and audience members can see you. Never stand or sit behind anything.
- *Move.* Move into your audience. Move around the room so that you include everyone in the group. But don't drift: move, and then pick a spot to stand for a while before moving again.

- *Don't turn your back on the audience.* Never talk facing away from your audience. Be especially aware of this if you are using projection or demonstrating with a computer monitor. If you must look at the projection or monitor, stop speaking, look at it, and then turn back to your audience and resume speaking.
- *Slow down.* Most people begin talking faster when they are nervous and/or when they feel a need to rush. Slow down. Come to full stops at the ends of sentences. Allow your audience to take in what you are saying. Breathe.

Nightmares in Training, or Murphy's Law

- *Questions you can't answer.* Don't try to cover up the fact that you don't know the answer. Acknowledge it. Depending on the question, your audience, and the time available, you can ask if anyone else in the group knows the answer; suggest resources where the answer may be found; offer to meet with the person after class; offer to do some research and get back to them at a later date.
- *Irrelevant questions.* Allow only enough time during the session as a question warrants. If a question is not relevant or of interest to the rest of the group, offer to meet with the person after class to discuss the issue.
- *Passive groups.* Direct questions to specific people. Have activities planned throughout the agenda. Break the group into small units for activities. Don't be afraid to lecture, if all else fails.
- *Disruptive groups.* Walk over and stand near the people who are being disruptive. Ask a disruptive pair or group if they have a question or something to share with the rest of the group. Ask chronic disrupters to leave.
- *Know-it-alls.* Acknowledge their contribution. If they really are knowledgeable, let them contribute their knowledge. But respect the rights of others to participate. Keep to the timed agenda. Do not call on only them.
- *Equipment failure.* Have nontechnical backups prepared, such as overheads or locally loaded files. Do not spend the entire session trying to fix the problem. Try for a few minutes and/ or have an assistant try to fix the problem. If it is not fixed after a few minutes, shrug if off and turn to the nontechnical backups.

RESOURCES FOR INTERNET TRAINERS

Books

Barclay, Donald, ed. *Teaching Electronic Information Literacy.* New York: Neal-Schuman Publishers, 1995.

> Covers a wide range of issues, from designing computer labs to teaching effectively.

Caroselli, Marlene. *Great Session Openers, Closers, and Energizers.* New York: McGraw-Hill, 1998.

> Emphasizes the importance of opening and closing training sessions on a high note.

Charles, C. Leslie. *The Instant Trainer: Quick Tips on How to Teach Others What You Know.* New York: McGraw-Hill, 1997.

> Offers a crash course for people who unexpectedly find themselves to be trainers.

Charney, Cyril, et al. *The Trainer's Toolkit.* New York: AMACOM, 1998.

> Provides information and guidance on 80 training topics.

Goad, Tom. *The First Time Trainer: A Step-by-Step Quick Guide for Managers, Supervisors, and New Training Professionals.* New York: AMACOM, 1997.

> Offers a concise guide with real-world examples.

LaGuardia, Cheryl, et al. *Teaching the New Library: A How-To-Do-It Manual for Planning and Designing Instructional Programs.* New York: Neal-Schuman Publishers, 1996.

> Covers library instruction issues in the electronic age.

Martin, Lyn Elizabeth M. *The Challenge of Internet Literacy: The Instruction-Web Convergence.* New York: Haworth Press, 1997.

> Includes examples of successful Web teaching programs.

Mitchell, Garry. *The Trainer's Handbook: The AMA Guide to Effective Training.* New York: AMACOM, 1998.

> Covers all aspects of training, from planning through delivery.

Newstrom, John W., and Edward E. Scannell. *Games Trainers Play.* New York: McGraw-Hill, 1980.

> Offers great ideas and examples. Also look for subsequent editions and similar titles.

Reichel, Mary, and Mary Ann Ramey. *Conceptual Frameworks for Bibliographic Education: Theory into Practice.* Littleton, Colo.: Libraries Unlimited, 1987.

> A classic in library instruction and learning theory.

Shonrock, Diana D. *Evaluating Library Instruction: Sample Questions, Forms, and Strategies for Practical Use.* Chicago: American Library Association, 1995.

> Provides practical guidance on evaluation techniques.

Silberman, Mel, et al. *101 Ways to Make Training Active.* Johannesburg; San Diego: Pfeiffer, 1995.

> Includes adaptable ideas for in-class exercises.

Van Kavelaar, Eileen K. *Conducting Training Workshops: A Crash Course for Beginners.* San Francisco: Jossey-Bass Publishers, 1997.

> Offers practical help for new trainers.

INTERNET TRAIN THE TRAINERS—(CONTINUED)

Periodicals

Training.

    A monthly magazine covering workplace training issues.

Training and Development Journal.

    A monthly journal from the American Society for Training and Development (ASTD), covering a wide variety of training issues. Also look for books published by ASTD.

Web Sites

ACRL Instruction Section

    http://www.lib.utexas.edu/is/

    A section of the Association of College and Research Libraries devoted to library instruction. Information on conferences, awards, publications, and committees.

ASTD: American Society for Training and Development

    http://www.astd.org/

    Includes information about the association, discussion forums, and links to other training resources.

CompuTouch's Suggestions for Computer Based Presentations

    http://www.computouch.ca/present.htm

    Provides tips on using LCD panels and data projectors for presentations.

ICONnect: Online Courses

    http://www.ala.org/ICONN/onlineco.html

    From the American Association of School Librarians (AASL). Includes adaptable training courses.

Internet Tutorials

    http://www.albany.edu/library/internet/

    From the State University of New York at Albany. A collection of online Internet lessons.

NetLearn

    http://www.rgu.ac.uk/~sim/research/netlearn/callist.htm

    Offers a directory of resources for anyone who teaches about or uses the Internet.

NETTRAIN

    http://lawlib.slu.edu/faculty/milles/nettrain/

    A discussion list specifically for Internet trainers.

net.Tutor

    http://gateway.lib.ohio-state.edu/tutor/

    From Ohio State University. Includes a variety of interactive Internet tutorials.

The Scout Toolkit

    http://wwwscout.cs.wisc.edu/scout/toolkit/

    Includes links to many Internet resources for searching, creating, and staying current.

ZA
4201
HeS
1999

Teaching the Internet to library staff + users

The Technology Resource Institute
   http://www.tripl.org/
   Includes Web-based training materials and other resources.
TRDEV-L
   http://train.ed.psu.edu/trdev-l/
   A discussion list on training and development for human resource professionals.
Walt Howe's Internet Learning Center
   http://people.ne.mediaone.net/walthowe/index.html
   Offers a collection of sample workshops and links to other resources.

INTERNET WORKSHOP EVALUATION FORM

Workshop Title: _____ Today's Date:_____

For each of the following areas, please indicate your reaction:

Content	Excellent	Good	Needs Improvement	Not Applicable
Covered Useful Material	[ ]	[ ]	[ ]	[ ]
Practical to My Needs and Interests	[ ]	[ ]	[ ]	[ ]
Well Organized	[ ]	[ ]	[ ]	[ ]
Presented at the Right Level	[ ]	[ ]	[ ]	[ ]
Effective Activities	[ ]	[ ]	[ ]	[ ]
Useful Visual Aids and Handouts	[ ]	[ ]	[ ]	[ ]

Presentation	Excellent	Good	Needs Improvement	Not Applicable
Trainer's Knowledge of Material	[ ]	[ ]	[ ]	[ ]
Trainer's Presentation Style	[ ]	[ ]	[ ]	[ ]
Trainer Covered Material Clearly	[ ]	[ ]	[ ]	[ ]
Trainer Responded Well to Questions	[ ]	[ ]	[ ]	[ ]

How could this workshop be improved?

What other training workshops would you like to see the library offer?

Any other comments or suggestions?

Overall, how would you evaluate this training session?

Excellent	Good	Fair	Poor
[ ]	[ ]	[ ]	[ ]

4

Getting Started on the World Wide Web

*Handouts for this workshop
follow page 62.*

OVERVIEW

Who

The audience for this workshop is adults who have little or no experience with the Internet or the World Wide Web. Indeed, the trainees may have little or no experience using computers. Alternately, they may have some experience with the Web but want to fill in gaps in knowledge through a more formal training session. While designed for public library patrons, this workshop could easily be adapted for employees, as well as patrons of other kinds of libraries—really, anyone. This is a basic introduction; there is no prerequisite.

What

This customizable, ready-to-run workshop is a first introduction to the World Wide Web. It offers background information about the Internet, along with practical training on how to use the browser and search for information. The main focus is on the Web and on using the Web at the library, rather than on other Internet functions or on obtaining access at home or work.

Where

This workshop is designed as a lecture/demonstration, either for a small group (two to eight people) gathered around one computer, or using a computer and projector for a larger audience. However, this workshop often involves volunteers from the audience, and it could easily be adapted to a lab setting, with participants working along with the instructor.

When

This workshop is an hour and a half. It is nearly impossible to give a meaningful introduction to the Web in only an hour. As it is, this workshop is packed, but all of the information is truly essential to understanding the Web.

Why

The objectives of this workshop are for the trainees to be able to (1) explain what the World Wide Web is and what kinds of information are available on it; (2) use the browser to navigate or "surf" the Web; and (3) search the Web for information on a topic of interest.

WORKSHOP AGENDA

This agenda is crowded, but it is important to cover it all. Because the plan is so full, it may be necessary to maintain tight control of this class. For example, you may have to limit questions until the end. The class begins with approximately 15 minutes of lecture—more than one would often like—so it is important to get through it fairly quickly and proceed to the hands-on portions.

Attendees at this workshop may be particularly prone to insecurity about their lack of knowledge or experience with computers and the Internet; they may feel that everyone but them already knows about these things. It is important to be reassuring, down-to-earth, and enthusiastic. It is vital not to get bogged down in jargon; keep it simple and active. And beware of know-it-alls who try to dominate. Remember, this is a beginning class; focus the training on the beginners in the audience.

INTRODUCTION/OBJECTIVES (0:00–0:05)

- Welcome and introductions
- Objectives of the workshop—Trainees will be able to:
  1. Explain what the World Wide Web is and what kinds of information are available on it
  2. Use the browser to navigate or "surf" the Web
  3. Search the Web for information on a topic of interest

WHAT IS THE WORLD WIDE WEB? (0:05–0:10)

- A network of computers around the world, connected electronically by telephone lines, fiber-optic cables, and other links
- Includes text, graphics, sound, and video
- Uses point-and-click links to make searching easy
- Huge . . . and growing

WHAT INFORMATION CAN I FIND ON THE WEB? (0:10–0:15)

- Countless subjects and topics
- Information that is accurate and high quality
- Information that may not be accurate or authoritative
- Sites that may be offensive
- Only a portion of the information in the library

BROWSERS AND HOME PAGES (0:15–0:25)

- Browsers (e.g., Netscape Navigator and Microsoft Internet Explorer): display the text and the graphics
- Home page: introductory page for a Web site
- Mouse: practice scrolling and clicking

FOLLOWING LINKS (0:25–0:35)

- Text links: usually blue or purple, and underlined, but can be graphical. Look for the little hand!
- Tool bar buttons used for going back, forward, and home
- Stop button used if pages load too slowly

WEB ADDRESSES (OR URLs) (0:35–0:40)

- Definition: a unique address
- Explanation of parts of a URL

Going to a Known Site (0:40–0:50)

- Where to find Web addresses
- How to type in a Web address and connect to a site
- Error messages and what they can mean

Subject Indexes and Search Engines (0:50–1:05)

- Using them to explore and find information on a topic
- Using a subject index: Yahoo
- Using a search engine: AltaVista
- Finding subject indexes and search engines

Printing/Saving (1:05–1:15)

- Printing a document
- Using Print Preview
- Saving a document to disk

Evaluation of Web Resources (1:15–1:20)

- Why it's important: not all information accurate, authoritative, unbiased, current
- What to look for: domain, author/publisher, date, overall package

Signing Off

Review and Wrap Up

- Review
- Library procedures
- Handouts and further information
- Evaluation
- Thanks for coming

SAMPLE SCRIPT

The script is provided to give you ideas: language to use, analogies to make, ways to put across ideas, and so forth. You'll have to find your own personal style, and being true to that is the most important thing. Some points, of course, will have to be modified for your local situation. Illustrated in this script, however, are some general points to keep in mind:

- *Keep the language as simple and jargon-free as possible.*
- *Be reassuring and relaxed.*
- *Make it active and try to use volunteers.*

Introduction/Objectives (0:00–0:05)

Hello! Welcome to the library and to our "Getting Started on the World Wide Web" workshop. My name is [*your name*] and I am a librarian here at the [*your library*]. In the next hour, you are going to learn the practical basics of how to use and search the World Wide Web.

Before we begin, why don't we go around and introduce ourselves and say a little bit about our experience using computers and the Internet. And, by the way, it's just fine if you don't have any experience—this class is a beginning class. We're going to start with the basics!

> *[Introductions. This is optional and depends on your environment, the number of people in the group, and your comfort level with the audience. You—and your patrons—may prefer to be more anonymous. Nevertheless, even if you don't do introductions, it is a good idea to try and get some feedback on the experience and knowledge of your audience before you begin. You may want to ask for a show of hands to see who has used the Internet before. Or, even better, simply ask the group, "Has anyone used the Internet before?" Try to get a conversation going to warm up the group and get them relaxed and involved. You may also want to personalize and tell a story about your own experience learning to use computers and the Internet. Be encouraging and empathetic.]*

Thanks! And thanks for coming today. Please feel free to ask me any questions as we go along, or after class. I also really encourage you to come back any day we're open and use the Internet at the library. By far the best way to learn is to practice, practice, practice, and all of our staff members will be happy to help.

As I said, this is an introduction to the World Wide Web. And here is what you will be able to do at the end of this workshop:

- You will be able to explain what the World Wide Web is and what kinds of information are available on it.

- You will be able to use the computer to navigate or "surf" the Web.
- You will be able to search the Web for information on a topic that interests you.

So let's begin!

What Is the World Wide Web? (0:05–0:10)

We have all heard about it, read about it, but what exactly is the Internet? What is the World Wide Web?

Well, the Internet is a network made up of computers all over the world, connected electronically by telephone lines, fiber-optic cables, and other links. These computers, because they are connected this way, can share and exchange information. Some people call the Internet a "network of networks."

The Web is the part or service of the Internet that uses text, images, sound, and video. It links documents together so that just by using the computer mouse you can jump from document to document, even if the documents are on computers in different states or even different countries. This linking is sometimes called hypertext. This makes the Web fun and exciting, and also pretty easy to use.

The Web is only a few years old, but it's already huge, and it's growing every day. Currently, there are hundreds of thousands of Web sites, with tens of millions of pages of information.

What Information Can I Find on the Web? (0:10–0:15)

You can find something about just about any subject on the Web. The Web has great resources for job hunting, travel, news, entertainment, law, government, statistics, cooking, computers, health—you name it. All kinds of people and organizations put up information on the Web: government agencies, private companies, universities, nonprofit and social service organizations, small businesses, individuals of all kinds. A Web site might contain a company's product information, a schedule of lectures at a museum, a government manual, or an individual's personal opinions. The possibilities are endless. It's a wonderful information resource that brings the world to you.

However, there are a few things to be aware of in order to use this tool effectively:

Anyone can publish something on the Web. This means that, even more so than with books and magazines, you shouldn't believe everything you read. Not everything on the Web is accurate or authoritative. So it's important to evaluate the source of the information you find, and later we'll talk about some ways to do that.

This also means that there are things on the Web that you or I may find offensive. You may not stumble across these things if you're not looking for them, but it's important to know that they are there. And if you're a parent, it's important that you talk to your children, set rules, and monitor their use of the Internet.

[At this point, it may be a good idea to review the library's policy about Internet usage and children. It is also a good opportunity to highlight any positive steps the library is taking to educate children about the Internet: classes, brochures, library-created Web pages for children, and so forth.]

Finally, another important thing to keep in mind is that, even though the Web is huge and growing all the time, not everything can be found there, and probably never will be. You should still use all the other great resources at the library, like the books and the magazines and the CD-ROMs. Very often you'll have more luck using these more traditional resources, and a librarian can help you decide where to look for what you need. Often you'll want to check both print and computer resources. And remember, as with all good research, researching information on the Web can take some time. But we're going to learn some tips today for using your time on the Web most effectively.

Browsers and Home Pages (0:15–0:25)

You may have heard of Netscape Navigator and Microsoft Internet Explorer. These are known as browsers for the World Wide Web. There are also other browsers on the market. Basically, browsers are just the software programs that allow you to read and see the information and images on the Web. They provide the commands and the buttons you can click on. All browsers work pretty much the same; once you have used one, you can usually figure out how another is used. This library uses [*browser name*], which is what you see on the screen here. You can see the logo there in the upper right corner.

Browsers like Netscape or Internet Explorer are not the same things as online service providers or Internet service providers, such as America Online or CompuServe. You need to sign up with a service provider if you have a computer and modem and want to gain access to the Internet at home. If you sign up with one of these providers, they will give you a browser to use, like Netscape or Internet Explorer or maybe one of their own. We have more information about getting Internet access at home, and we can talk about that later.

You may have also heard the phrase "home page." Basically, a home page is just the introductory or first page of an organization or individual's Web site. A Web site can be thought of as a collection of pages of information stored on a particular computer. What you see here is the home page for [*name Web site*].

[You can choose any Web site to demonstrate first. It might be a good idea to use your library's own Web site, if it exists, since it may also be set as the default home page on your public access computers. If not, it would be good to choose either a major or a local company or organization—something that everyone in your audience will have heard of and may be interested in.]

I have been using the term "page," but a Web page can actually be more than one screen long and more than one page if you printed it out. To see everything on one page, you use the left button of the mouse to click on the bar along the right to scroll up and down. I can click on the up and down arrows to scroll slowly, or in between the box and the arrow to jump more quickly.

[Demonstrate.]

I can also hold the left mouse button down to move more quickly.

[Demonstrate. Another option is to take a few minutes and have everyone practice scrolling up and down. This will depend on the size of your group, but it's a good idea to get everyone's hands on the machine, if possible.]

One of the most important things to remember today is that you're not going to break the machine! Computers are pretty sturdy these days, so don't be afraid to move the mouse around or touch the keyboard. It can also take some time to get used to using the mouse. But don't get discouraged—it just takes a little practice and then you'll feel comfortable. By the way, you can also use the arrow keys and the Page Up and Page Down keys to move up and down.

[Demonstrate.]

Following Links (0:25–0:35)

One of the wonderful things about the Web is the way it allows you to follow links using the mouse. As I said, this is sometimes called hypertext and the links are sometimes called hyperlinks. Let's follow a link.

[Ask for a volunteer to operate the mouse. Another option is to do it yourself, but it is better to have a participant try it out, even though it may slow down the session.]

Notice these underlined words here, in blue. Let's move the mouse and put the arrow over one of those words. See how it turns into a little hand? That means we can use the left mouse button to click once on that text, and it will take us to a different page. Let's do that now.

[You or your volunteer clicks on a textual hyperlink.]

So, you see, that has taken us to a different page, which has more information and more links. Let's click on another link.

[You or your volunteer clicks on another textual hyperlink.]

So, again, that has taken us to another page.

By the way, if a link is purple, it means you've already been there—so it can be a good way to keep track of where you've been. But even though links are most often in blue or purple, they aren't always; they might be in any color. And they're not always text; they might be buttons [*point to a button*] or pictures or graphics of some kind. If the arrow turns into a hand when you drag it across a picture or some text then you know it's a link, and that you can click on it to go to another page. Let's try that now.

[You or your volunteer clicks on a graphical link. You will have to plan this in advance to make sure that the site you are using—and the page you will be on—has a graphical link.]

Now let's say you want to go back to the previous page and look at that again. Notice up here the Forward button and the Back button. We can't go forward yet because we haven't been anywhere else; notice that the button is faded to a much lighter shade of gray. But we can go back—that button is not faded. Let's do that now.

[You or your volunteer clicks on the Back button.]

So, you see, that brings us back to the previous page. Let's click Back again.

[You or your volunteer clicks on the Back button.]

And again.

[You or your volunteer clicks on the Back button, to return to the home page of the site.]

And that brings us back to the previous page, which is where we started. So this is how you can retrace your steps. Notice that we can now click the Forward button, too—it's not light gray anymore. Let's do that.

[You or your volunteer clicks on the Forward button.]

And then Back again.

[You or your volunteer clicks on the Back button, to return to the home page of the site.]

So we've learned how to identify text links—they are often in blue or purple, but can be in any color, and when you put the mouse pointer over it, the arrow turns into a little hand. We have also learned that links can be pictures or buttons, as well as text. Finally, we have learned how to use the Back and Forward buttons to go back and forth one page at a time, and we have returned to the home page of this Web site. Another tip is that you can always use the Home button here at the top to return to the home page for [*your library, or whatever home page is set as the default for your public access computers*].

Thanks to our volunteer!

[Have volunteer return to audience.]

By the way, another button here at the top is the Stop button. Sometimes pages can take a long time to load, or they get hung up for one reason or another. If that happens and you want to try something else, you can click the Stop button and that will usually stop it and you can move on.

OK, now I am moving my arrow over a link.

[Move arrow over a link.]

Look down here at the bottom of the screen. Notice that string of letters? That's a Web address. Another way to tell if something is a link is if, when you move the arrow over a word or a picture, an address that looks something like this appears at the bottom. That's the address for the page you will go to if you click on that link. And we are going to talk about Web addresses next.

Web Addresses (or URLs) (0:35–0:40)

Now, let's look up here in the location or address box. Notice that it says [*read the URL*]. This is the Web address for [*name the site—perhaps your library*]. These addresses are sometimes called URLs, which stands for Uniform Resource Locator and is usually pronounced by sounding out the three letters, U-R-L, or saying "Earl." You've probably seen addresses like this advertised on TV, in magazines and newspapers, on billboards, and other places.

There are a few important things to keep in mind about these addresses.

One is that they are unique. Nobody besides [*name the sponsor of the site you are using to demonstrate—perhaps your library*] has this address, and when you type that address in, this is the only place you'll ever go. It's like a telephone number, or a postal address.

When you connect to an address, you are going over telecommunications lines (like telephone lines), contacting the computer (called the server) with that unique address, and that computer is serving up the Web page and sending it back to your machine. That server you are connecting to could be in another part of the same building, around the block, or around the world. It doesn't really matter, and you usually won't know.

You'll also notice that the Web address has sections separated by periods (people call them "dots" when they are talking about Web addresses), colons, and slashes. Let's look at the different elements of a Web address.

The part before the colon and two slashes—*http*—stands for hypertext transfer protocol. That's a technical protocol, and it's not really important to know what that means, but all Web site addresses start with that. The part after the two slashes is the address for the computer you are contacting; it's the main part of the address. Often the first part will start with *www*, but not always. The middle part will often be the name of the company or organization you're trying to reach, but not always. [*Use the address of the site you are using to illustrate.*]

The last part is the domain or category of the site. [*Use the address of the site you are using to illustrate. For example: "Here it is .org, which stands for organization and is used for nonprofit organizations, like the library."*] Other common ones you'll see are *.com* for commercial businesses (like *http://www.ibm.com/*), *.edu* for educational institutions (like *http://www.harvard.edu/*). and *.gov* for government agencies (like *http://www.fbi.gov/*). Sites from other countries will have different extensions, like *.fr* for France and *.uk* for the United Kingdom.

Sections of the URL that follow this main part of the Web address often follow more slashes and represent other subsections within that Web site. For instance, when I go forward to a page we have already seen, notice that the Web address gets longer and has more slashes.

[*Click Forward and Back, to illustrate.*]

Going to a Known Site (0:40–0:50)

One way to locate information on the Web is to go to a site you already have the address for. Where are some places you can find addresses?

[*Get responses. If not, supply them.*]

Great! So some of the places you can find addresses are:

- Friends and colleagues
- Magazines and newspapers
- Television
- Directories (like the *Internet Yellow Pages*) and others books here at the library
- Handouts (I have some that I will give out at the end of the workshop)
- Guessing

[Ask: Can anyone guess the URL for Ford Motor Company? (Or use another site that would be easy to guess.)]

Let's go to a site I know the address for.

[Ask for another volunteer (someone new).]

There are a few different ways to type in an address. One is just to click on the Open button at the top and type in the address. Another is to go under File/Open Location. [Demonstrate File pulldown menu.] The way I like to do it is just to type it into the location or address box. Let's do that.

There are a few important things to keep in mind, though, when you are typing in the address:

- You have to type in the address exactly, paying attention to upper and lower cases, slashes, dots, etc. If you make any mistake, it won't work and you'll get an error message.
- The *http://* part of the Web address is usually optional; you can either type it in or leave it out. Most browsers today take for granted that the address you're going to type in begins with *http://*, and they will put it in for you. So I usually leave it out.
- There will usually be a previous address already in the box. You'll have to get rid of that one before you type in the new one. The easiest way to do that is to click once in the box. That will highlight the address. Then, you can hit the Backspace or Delete key, or you can just start typing in the new address and the old one will disappear.

Here's an address I know by heart.

[Have some sites handy, and pick one that you think your audience might find interesting—either a well-known or a local organization. Some sites that might work well are:
http://www.switchboard.com/

> http://www.careerpath.com/
> http://www.cnn.com/
> http://www.amazon.com/
> http://www.collegeboard.org/
> http://www.nasa.gov/
> http://www.stanford.edu/
> *You or your volunteer connects to that site.]*

Now, this time watch the icon in the upper right corner and also how the arrow turns into an hourglass.

[You or your volunteer connects to another site.]

This means that the computer is trying to make the connection, and you shouldn't keep clicking the mouse—that can cause the computer to freeze up. It sometimes just takes a little time to connect. If it's taking too much time, remember you can always click on the Stop button to stop the search.

Now, this time watch along the bottom of the screen for messages. This will also tell you that the computer is trying to make the connection.

[You or your volunteer connects to another site.]

By the way, if you get an error message, it might mean one of a few things: you may have made a typo in the Web address; the computer you are trying to contact may be temporarily busy or out of commission; or the address you have may be incorrect or out-of-date. That can happen—Web addresses sometimes change. One of the frustrating things about the Web is that sometimes there's no way to know precisely what's causing an error message. Double-check the address you typed in, try again, and if it still sends back an error, wait and try that site again later in your session.

Now we know how to locate Web addresses, and how to type in an address and go to a site. But what if you just want to explore a topic or area, and don't have a specific site in mind? We'll turn to that next.

Thanks to our volunteer!

[Have volunteer return to seat.]

Subject Indexes and Search Engines (0:50–1:05)

When you are interested in exploring a topic or subject, but you don't know any specific sites to start with or places to go, you need to use what are called subject indexes and search engines. These are Web sites that allow you to browse the Web by subject or to type in words or a phrase to search.

Let's start with subject indexes.

[Ask for another volunteer (someone new).]

The best-known example of a subject index is one called Yahoo. Has anyone heard of Yahoo? Let's go there.

[You or your volunteer types in the address for Yahoo—http://www.yahoo.com/]

Notice how this works. Yahoo has Web sites arranged by subject, with major subject categories, and then subcategories underneath.

[You or your volunteer do a sample search. It is crucial to plan your search in advance, and check it right before class to avoid last-minute surprises. Two sample searches that work well in Yahoo are:

- *Recreation and Sports*
- *Sports*
- *Basketball*
- *National Basketball Association*
- *NBA.com (http://www.nba.com/)*

and

- *Education*
- *Financial Aid*
- *FinAid: The Financial Aid Information Page (http://www.finaid.com/)*

Optional: After your prepared search, you may also wish to ask the audience if there is something they are interested in, and do a search on that. That approach has the advantage of helping to keep them engaged. However, it can take up valuable time, and success is uncertain.]

Subject indexes are really useful if you want to browse and see what is available on a particular subject. They are sort of like using the library's old card catalog and looking books up by subject. Or they are like going to the shelf and browsing the books there on a particular topic.

Thanks to our volunteer!

[Have volunteer return to seat.]

The other way to search for information on the Web is to use a keyword search engine.

[Ask for another volunteer (someone new).]

There are many different search engines and they all work in somewhat similar ways. One that I like is AltaVista. Let's go there.

[You or your volunteer types in address for AltaVista—http://www.altavista.digital.com/]

As you see, there's a box here where you can type in key words or a phrase. You can just click in the box and type in words to search for. Or, in AltaVista, if you want to search a phrase, you put it in quotation marks.

[You or your volunteer does a sample search. Again, it is crucial to plan your search in advance, and check it right before class to avoid last-minute surprises. These two sample searches work well in AltaVista. Type in: chocolate chip cookies recipe or a line from a poem or song, such as "shall I compare thee to a summer's day?"]

As you see, AltaVista has searched the Web for these words and brought back a list of Web sites, which you can then click on and go to. Keyword search engines like this are particularly good for finding very specific or obscure information.

When you're using search engines, it's important to read the help screens and try to narrow your search to the most specific search you can. This will help you to get more relevant results.

[Optional: Again, after your prepared search, if there is time, you may also wish to ask the audience if there is something they are interested in and do a search on that. The same advantages and dangers apply.]

Thanks to our volunteer!

[Have volunteer return to seat.]

So, to recap: Subject indexes like Yahoo are good for browsing a topic and beginning your search. Keyword search engines like AltaVista are good for very specialized or esoteric questions.

[At this point, it would be a good idea to mention how to find these and other indexes and search engines. Tell them that they can type in addresses directly, as we have done here. Also mention how to get lists of indexes and search engines: for example, from the library Web page, from handouts, from the Search button of the browser.

It's also good at this point to refer participants to any more advanced workshops you may be offering on using searching engines and indexes. See "Using Search Engines and Finding Information" in Chapter 5.]

Printing and Saving (1:05–1:15)

[Go to a Web page that is multiple screens long.]

Just one more practical tip. You'll probably want to print some of the documents you find. There's an easy way to do that: just click on the Print button here at the top.

However, as we've learned, sometimes a Web page can, in fact, be many screens long, and if you just click the Print button, it will print the entire document. That can sometimes be as many as 50 pages or more! For example, if I scroll down this site, you can see it would be many pages long if I printed it out. You might not want to print the whole thing. A handy trick is to select only the pages you want to print.

[Demonstrate how to select print options using the File/Print command and do a sample printout. You might want to mention other incentives for printing only selected pages—for example, if your library charges for printing. Review any other library printing policies.]

Another option, if you have a computer at home, work, or school, is to save a Web page to disk.

[Demonstrate how to download information using the File/Save As command. Be sure to cover the selection of drive and file type (HTML or Text). Review any other library downloading policies, such as the use or purchase of floppy disks.]

Evaluation of Web Resources (1:15–1:20)

Remember we said that anyone can publish on the Web. As you search around using some of the tools we've just learned about today, you'll come across a lot of different sites, some of which will have good, authoritative information, and some of which won't. It's important to evaluate the information you find, but that's not always so easy to do.

One thing to look at is the Web address or URL. Is it a .gov site, meaning it comes from the government? Is it a .com site, meaning it's operated by a business or commercial service? Sometimes, looking at the URL doesn't give you much to go on, though. For instance, an .edu education page could be a professor's work or an individual student's personal page.

It's important to look at the name of the organization in conjunction with the URL. Is it an organization or company that you have heard of? Is it an authority on the topic covered in the Web site? If the site is done by an individual, look for information about that individual; sometimes individuals will put up information about themselves, their background, and their credentials.

Another thing to look for is a date. Often sites will give the last date that a page was updated. Some sites are not updated for years, and some are updated many times a day. This is more or less important depending on the kind of site it is and the kind of information it presents. A news site should be updated constantly. An essay on Shakespeare may never need to be updated.

Finally, it's important to look at the overall package. Do all of the factors indicate that this is an authoritative, official site?

SIGN OFF

One last thing: When you are finished, it's important to exit the system properly.

[Demonstrate how to exit the browser and any other library sign-off procedures.]

Review and Wrap Up (1:20–1:30)

We have covered a lot of material today. Let's just quickly review:

We have learned that the Internet is a collection of computers all over the world, connected electronically by telecommunications wires in order to share and exchange information. The World Wide Web is the part of the Internet that uses hypertext links for navigation. It has wonderful information on all topics, but not everything can be found on the Web and not all the information found on the Web is accurate.

We have learned to use the keyboard and mouse to scroll up and down the screen, to click on links, and to navigate or surf the Web using the [*name of browser*] browser.

We have learned how to begin searching the Web for information. We have learned that there are basically two types of search services: subject indexes like Yahoo and keyword search engines like AltaVista.

As I said earlier, the best way to continue to learn more about the Web is to use it. We provide it here for *you* to use. So please take advantage of it! Here are our procedures:

[Review available times, sign-up procedures, etc.]

Another good way to learn is by reading. We have a number of books and magazines about the Internet here at the library, both for reference and for circulation.

[It is a good idea to have some books and magazines from the collection on hand to show. You might want to mention where they are located.]

We have also developed some handouts for you to take and use. These review a lot of the things we covered today, and also have some pointers to more information.

[Distribute handouts [pages 63-68]. Also mention any further training workshops upcoming in the library.]

Are there any final questions?

Please always feel free to ask me or the other staff members here any questions you may have in the future. Thanks so much for coming!

[If you are taking evaluations (either the one on page 44 or on your own), you will want to distribute them and ask the group to fill them out. You may also want to schedule some practice time on the machines for the participants. This would be an excellent way for them to reinforce immediately what they have learned.]

GETTING STARTED ON THE WORLD WIDE WEB AGENDA

Introduction/Objectives

- Welcome and introductions
- Objectives of the workshop—
  1. Explain what the World Wide Web is and what kinds of information are available on it
  2. Use browser to navigate or "surf" the Web
  3. Search the Web for information on topic of interest

What Is the World Wide Web?

- A network of computers around the world, connected electronically by telephone lines, fiber-optic cables, and other links
- Includes text, graphics, sound, and video
- Uses point-and-click links to make searching easy
- Huge . . . and growing

What Information Can I Find on the Web?

- Countless subjects and topics
- Information that is accurate and high quality
- Information that may not be accurate or authoritative
- Sites that may be offensive
- Only a portion of the information in the library

Browers and Home Pages

- Browers (e.g., Netscape and Internet Explorer): display the text and the graphics
- Home page: introductory page for a Web site
- Mouse: practice scrolling and clicking

Following Links

- Text links: usually blue or purple, and underlined, but can be graphical. Look for the little hand!
- Tool bar button used for going back, forward, and home
- Stop button used if pages load too slowly

Web Addresses (or URLs)

- Definition: a unique address
- Explanation of parts of a URL

Going to a Known Site

- Where to find Web addresses
- How to type in a Web address and connect to a site
- Error messages and what they can mean

GETTING STARTED ON THE WORLD WIDE WEB AGENDA—(CONTINUED)

Subject Indexes and Search Engines

- Using them to explore and find information on a topic
- Using a subject index: Yahoo
- Using a search engine: AltaVista
- Finding subject indexes and search engines

Printing/Saving

- Printing a document
- Using Print Preview
- Saving a document to disk

Evaluation of Web Resources

- Why it's important: not all information accurate, authoritative, unbiased, current
- What to look for: domain, author/publisher, date, overall package

Signing Off

Review and Wrap Up

- Library procedures
- Handouts and further information
- Evaluation
- Thanks for coming

GETTING STARTED ON THE WORLD WIDE WEB: KEY POINTS

THE BASICS

What Is the Internet? What Is the World Wide Web?

The Internet is a collection of computers all over the world, connected electronically by telecommunications lines in order to share and exchange information. The World Wide Web is the part of the Internet that uses hypertext links for navigation; it includes text, graphics, video, and sound. The Web has wonderful information on just about any topic, but not everything can be found on the Web and not all the information found on the Web is accurate.

How Do I "Surf" the Web?

Use the mouse, the keyboard, and the browser (for example, Netscape Navigator or Microsoft Internet Explorer) to scroll up and down the screen, to click on textual and graphical links, and to navigate or surf the Web. Here are the main buttons of the browser and what they do:
- Back: Takes you back one Web page at a time.
- Forward: Takes you forward one Web page at time.
- Home: Takes you "home"—to the first Web page.
- Stop: Stops a search in progress.
- Print: Prints the Web page you are looking at.

How Do I Find Information on a Topic that Interests Me?

If you know a good site to start with, type the Web address (URL) directly into the address or location box of the browser. If you don't, then use subject indexes and search engines. Use subject indexes like Yahoo (*http://www.yahoo.com/*) to browse for information and sites on particular topics. Use keyword search engines like AltaVista (*http://www.altavista.digital.com/*) to search for specific and/or obscure information.

How Do I Get Internet Access at Home?

You will need a computer, a modem (which allows your computer to use the telephone line to connect to the Internet), and an Internet Service Provider (ISP). In most cases, you pay the ISP a monthly access fee—usually about $10 to $20 per month. An extensive directory of ISPs can be found on the Web at The List: The Definitive ISP Buyer's Guide (*http://thelist.internet.com/*). Other options are also becoming available, such as WebTV. Your local computer dealership should be able to help you.

GETTING STARTED ON THE WORLD WIDE WEB

A FEW USEFUL WEB SITES

Yahoo
http://www.yahoo.com/
AltaVista
http://www.altavista.digital.com/
Switchboard
http://www.switchboard.com/
CareerPath.com
http://www.careerpath.com/
CNN Interactive
http://www.cnn.com/
College Board Online
http://www.collegeboard.com/
NASA
http://www.nasa.gov/
NBA.com
http://www.nba.com/
IBM
http://www.ibm.com/
Federal Bureau of Investigation (FBI)
http://www.fbi.gov/
Harvard University
http://www.harvard.edu/
FinAid: The Financial Aid Information Page
http://www.finaid.com/
Amazon.com
http://www.amazon.com/
LatinoLink
http://www.latinolink.com/
FindLaw: Internet Legal Resources
http://www.findlaw.com/
Women's Wire
http://www.womenswire.com/
The American Association of Retired Persons (AARP)
http://www.aarp.org/
The Internet Movie Database
http://www.imdb.com/

Resources for Parents and Kids (maintained by the American Library Association)
    http://www.ala.org/parents/index.html
Librarians' Index to the Internet
    http://sunsite.berkeley.edu/InternetIndex/

FURTHER READING AND RESOURCES

Listed below are just a few of the many available books, periodicals, and Web sites about the Internet and the World Wide Web. Please consult the library's catalog or ask a librarian for more recommendations.

Books

December, John. *The World Wide Web Unleashed.* Indianapolis, Ind.: Sams, 1997.
    An extensive reference work covering all aspects of the World Wide Web.
Habraken, Joe. *The Big Basics Book of the Internet.* Indianapolis, Ind.: Que Education and Training, 1997.
    Illustrated lessons for the new Internet user.
Internet Yellow Pages. 6th ed. Indianapolis, Ind.: New Riders Publishing, 1997.
    An annotated directory of thousands of Web sites.
Levine, John R., et al. *The Internet for Dummies.* 5th ed. Foster City, Calif.: IDG Books Worldwide, 1998.
    A plain-English introduction to the Internet and the World Wide Web.
Ross, John. *Discover the World Wide Web.* Foster City, Calif.: IDG Books Worldwide, 1997.
    An introduction with pointers to valuable Web sites in a variety of categories.
Whitehead, Paul, and Ruth Maran. *Internet and World Wide Web: Simplified.* 2nd ed. Foster City, Calif.: IDG Books Worldwide, 1997.
    An introduction to the Internet. For beginners.

Periodicals

Net Guide Magazine.
    Includes Web site reviews and other features. Online version available at *http://www.netguide.com/*.
PC World.
    Provides coverage of Internet issues and products, as well as PC product reviews. Online version available at *http://www.pcworld.com/*.
Wired.
    Offers feature articles and commentary on technology and online culture. Online version available at *http://www.wired.com/wired/*. See also *Hotwired* (*http://www.hotwired.com/*).
Yahoo! Internet Life.
    Provides Web site reviews and searching tips. Online version available at *http://www.zdnet.com/yil/*.

GETTING STARTED ON THE WORLD WIDE WEB—(CONTINUED)

Web Sites

Finding Information on the Internet: A Tutorial
> *http://www.lib.berkeley.edu/TeachingLib/Guides/Internet/FindInfo.html*
> From the University of California at Berkeley. An online introduction to the Web.

Internet Tutorials
> *http://www.albany.edu/library/internet/*
> From the University at Albany, State University of New York. A collection of online Internet lessons.

net. Tutor
> *http://gateway.lib.ohio-state.edu/tutor/*
> From Ohio State University. Includes a variety of interactive Internet tutorials.

Internet para empezar
> *http://www.cecafi.unam.mx/internet/*
> An introduction to the Internet in Spanish.

NetLingo: The Internet Language Dictionary
> *http://www.netlingo.com/*
> An online glossary of Internet terms.

CNET.COM
> *http://www.cnet.com/*
> Current news and information about computers, technology, and the Internet.

Internet Histories
> *http://www.isoc.org/internet-history/*
> From the Internet Society. Includes "A Brief History of the Internet" and a timeline.

5
Using Search Engines and Finding Information on the Web

Handouts for this workshop follow page 83.

OVERVIEW

Who

The prerequisite for this workshop is the "Getting Started on the World Wide Web" workshop. You may choose to open this workshop to adults who have not taken that workshop, but they must already have a basic understanding of how to navigate the Web. They must also have basic mouse and keyboard abilities. While designed for adult patrons of a public library, this workshop can be adapted easily to customers of other kinds of libraries.

What

This customizable, ready-to-run workshop builds on the fundamentals of the "Getting Started on the World Wide Web" workshop. It focuses on searching the Web for information. It covers subject directories and search engines, as well as other techniques. The workshop is hands-on; it encourages the participants to begin using the tools learned to search immediately for the information they need.

Where

This workshop is designed for a computer lab where the students can get hands-on experience searching for information. However, the lesson plan can also be used for a lecture or demonstration.

When

This workshop lasts for an hour and a half. Because it is largely hands-on, the time will go quickly. If you need to shorten the session, omit the second keyword search engine.

Why

The objectives of this workshop are for the trainees to be able to (1) explain the two major types of search services available for the Web; (2) decide which service(s) to use for which types of information needs; and (3) perform effective searches using a variety of specific tools.

WORKSHOP AGENDA

Again, this is a tight schedule. If you get behind and have to jettison something on the fly, omit the second search engine (HotBot). Since this is a hands-on class, it would help (although it's not necessary) to have an assistant, who can assist anyone who gets stuck and falls behind.

INTRODUCTION

- Welcome (0:00–0:01)
- Prerequisites (0:01–0:03)
- Objectives (0:03–0:05)

SUBJECT DIRECTORIES

- Introduction (0:05–0:10)
- Librarians' Index to the Internet (*http://sunsite.berkeley.edu/ InternetIndex/*)
  1. Overview (0:10–0:15)
  2. Sample Search (0:15–0:20)
  3. Audience Suggestion (0:20–0:25)
- Yahoo (*http://www.yahoo.com/*)
  1. Overview (0:25–0:30)
  2. Sample Search (0:30–0:35)
  3. Individual Searches (0:35–0:40)

SEARCH ENGINES

- Introduction (0:40–0:45)
- AltaVista (*http://altavista.digital.com/*)
  1. Overview (0:45–0:50)
  2. Sample Search (0:50–1:00)
  3. Audience Suggestion (1:00–1:05)
- HotBot (*http://www.hotbot.com/*)
  1. Overview (1:05–1:10)
  2. Sample Search (1:10–1:15)
  3. Individual Searches (1:15–1:20)

OTHER METHODS

- Other Search Engines (1:20–1:22)
- Starting with a Site You Know (1:22–1:25)

REVIEW (1:25–1:30)

SAMPLE SCRIPT

Unlike "Getting Started on the World Wide Web," this session is designed to be primarily hands-on. It is important, therefore, that you emphasize that "Getting Started on the World Wide Web" is a prerequisite for this workshop, and that if trainees haven't taken it, they must already be competent in basic computer and Web navigation skills. Otherwise, one person can hold up the entire group. Also, when you are conducting a hands-on workshop, you must be very clear about when the trainees should be practicing on their machines and when they should just watch. Be explicit about it; say, "OK, everybody take your hands off the keyboards and just watch me now," or "OK, everybody do this along with me." You will sometimes have to fight for their attention if they have the Web on their screens right in front of them.

Introduction

WELCOME (0:00–0:01)

Hello! Welcome to "Using Search Engines and Finding Information." Today we are going to learn how to become expert searchers of the Web.

PREREQUISITES (0:01–0:03)

Everyone here should already have taken our "Getting Started on the World Wide Web" workshop. If you haven't taken that workshop, you must already have a basic understanding of the Internet and how to navigate the Web. Everyone must also have basic mouse and keyboard skills, since this is going to be a real hands-on class. Is anyone in the wrong place, or does anybody have any questions about that?

OBJECTIVES (0:03–0:05)

Today's workshop is going to last an hour and a half. And we have three main objectives for this workshop.

> *[Have the three objectives already written on the board or flip chart, and reveal them at this time.]*

At the end of this workshop you will be able to (1) explain the two major types of search services available for the Web; (2) decide which service(s) to use for which types of information needs; and (3) perform effective searches using a variety of specific tools.

We're going to cover a lot of ground in this class, so let's begin!

Subject Directories

INTRODUCTION (0:05–0:10)

One way to find information on the Web is to use a site that categorizes resources by subject. If you want to see what's available on, say, dogs, then you can go to the Dogs category and browse to see what's available. We introduced one of these subject directories—Yahoo—in "Getting Started on the World Wide Web," and we are going to go back to Yahoo again in a few minutes. But first I want to show you another subject directory.

LIBRARIANS' INDEX TO THE INTERNET
(http://sunsite.berkeley.edu/InternetIndex/)

Overview (0:10–0:15)

Let's all go to a site called the Librarians' Index to the Internet.

> *[Click on the link, or have everyone type in the address with you. The Librarians' Index to the Internet is an excellent example of a selective directory of evaluated Web resources. If your library maintains such a directory of its own, you should demonstrate that one instead, as the resources will have been selected with the interests of your patrons in mind. Or, better yet, demonstrate both your local directory and the Librarians' Index to the Internet; you can either extend the session by 15 minutes, or cut one of the search engines from the workshop.]*

Is everybody there? Now let's take a look at this page for a minute. As you see, it looks kind of like Yahoo, with subject categories you can click on. The difference is that this directory is very selective in the sites that it includes. It only includes a few thousand sites, not hundreds of thousands. And these sites have been selected by librarians for their potential usefulness; they have been judged to be the most authoritative, comprehensive, and useful sites on their particular subjects.

Sample Search (0:15–0:20)

Let's select one of the categories. Let's try Automobiles—everyone please click on that. Here you see that, if you scroll down, the librarians have selected what they consider to be the best automobile sites on the Web, and they have given us short descriptions of what can be found at each site. They have even selected their "best of the best" at the top. Here you have Edmund's Automobile Buyer's Guide, the Kelley Blue Book, Microsoft CarPoint—some of the major car sites, where you can learn about new and used cars, get prices, and so forth.

Now let's click the Back button and go back to the home page for the Librarians' Index to the Internet.

Notice that, in addition to browsing by category, you can also use the search box up here. You can click in the box and type in a word or words. It won't search the whole Web, just the titles, annotations, and subjects of the resources selected here. So this search feature can also be useful if you're not sure what category something might be in, and there are search tips provided, as well.

Audience Suggestion (0:20–0:25)

Why don't we try to use the Librarians' Index to the Internet to look for something that somebody is interested in. Does anyone have anything—a subject or a site or a question—you'd like to look for?

> *[Get a suggestion from the audience. If no one volunteers, try to call on someone who looks willing to participate. When you receive a suggestion, try to find the answer or the resource using the Librarians' Index to the Internet, and explain why you are searching the way you are (that is, the category you are using, or, if you choose, the search feature). Also, consider asking the other participants—or even the person who made the suggestion—how they might go about looking for this. If you have time, do more than one sample search. Try to make the searches successful, or at least explain why they may not be successful with this resource. You may suggest returning to the question later, when you are covering keyword search engines.]*

The Librarians' Index to the Internet is an excellent place to begin your search. It is selective, it has great sites, and it is easy to use. You may not have to go any further. But because it is selective, it doesn't have everything and you may have to turn to other resources. We're going to look at Yahoo next. Are there any questions about the Librarians' Index to the Internet, before we move on?

Yahoo (*http://www.yahoo.com/*)

Overview (0:25–0:30)

OK, now let's all go to Yahoo.

> *[Click on the link, or have everyone type in the address with you.]*

We all talked about Yahoo in the "Getting Started on the World Wide Web" class, so you are already at least a little familiar with it. Like the Librarians' Index to the Internet, it has Internet resources arranged under subject categories. But there are a few differences.

One difference is that Yahoo has a lot of other features. You see it has news headlines and stories, sports news, yellow pages, white pages, games, stock quotes, an e-mail service—lots of other features besides the Internet directory.

And the difference between the Yahoo Internet directory and the Librarians' Index to the Internet is that Yahoo has a lot more stuff—hundreds of thousands of sites, as opposed to just a few thousand. Now that can be a good thing or a bad thing, depending on the circumstances. Why do you think that is?

[Get responses.]

There are more sites here, but they are not really selected for their usefulness—just about any site can get listed in Yahoo. So there will be a lot of not-so-great stuff in with the good stuff. It means that there is more to wade through, and that can make the search process more difficult and time-consuming.

The advantages are that you will find things here that are not listed in the Librarians' Index to the Internet. Also, different kinds of sites are here: more commercial sites, more individual home pages. And Yahoo does review some of the sites, and sometimes indicates ones they think are the best.

Sample Search (0:30–0:35)

So let's try our Automobiles search again. Here is the category. Let's everybody click on that.

And then, you see, it takes us to another page of subcategories, rather than the relatively short list of sites that the Librarians' Index to the Internet gave us. And the numbers in parentheses indicate the number of sites listed under each subcategory, so you can see there are a lot of sites here.

Let's click on the subcategory Buyer's Guides. There are quite a few sites here, but Yahoo provides reviews of a few; in addition, the sunglasses indicate the sites they select as the best. And here we see some of our old friends: Edmund's Automobile Buyer's Guide, Kelley Blue Book, Microsoft CarPoint. And you have a lot more sites listed here, with brief annotations. Some of these might prove useful to you, too.

Let's click back to the Yahoo home page and do one more quick search together, and then I'm going to let you search around a little on your own.

Let's say you're interested in buying a computer. Let's all click on Computers and the Internet. Now let's click on the subcategory Personal Computers. Here, you see, we can get things like reviews, computer magazines, user groups. Let's go to Manufacturers. And here, you see, you can get links to the computer manufacturers' Web sites, like Dell or Compaq or Gateway or IBM, where you can get information about their products and probably even purchase a personal computer online, if you wish. And there are smaller companies here, too. You probably wouldn't find these commercial sites all listed on the Librarians' Index to the Internet, which would focus more on sites for product reviews and reference information.

Individual Searches (0:35–0:40)

Now let's all click back to the Yahoo home page. We're going to take about five minutes to let you explore Yahoo on your own for anything you're interested in. I'm going to walk around—feel free to ask me anything, if you get stuck or have a question. Explore the Internet directory, and also the other features of Yahoo—like the news headlines—if you wish. You might want to hold off on the search box at the top, though, because we're going to cover that afterward.

[Individual searching time. Circulate and provide assistance as necessary.]

OK, any impressions from searching around Yahoo that you'd like to share? Things that seemed to work well?

[Discuss searching experiences for a minute or two.]

The last thing with Yahoo I'd like to show you is that search feature at the top. As with the Librarians' Index to the Internet, this will search the directory of Yahoo itself—the categories, the titles of the sites, and the annotations. This feature can help if you are looking for something specific—like a company name or an organization—but you don't know what category it's under, or you don't want to wade through the categories. For instance, if I type in *Compaq*, it is going to return all the Yahoo categories that have that word, and then all the sites. This can be a pretty good way of finding something quickly in Yahoo.

But let's say the word you type in doesn't appear at all in Yahoo. I'm going to do a nonsense search just to demonstrate. Let's say I add a *u* and type in *Compaqu*. What happens is that, when it doesn't find that word anywhere in Yahoo, it performs the search in AltaVista, which is a keyword search engine that searches the entire Web for that word. And, you see, it came back with some hits (but not in English, of course, since it's not an English word!) We are going to turn to AltaVista and go there directly next.

Search Engines

INTRODUCTION (0:40–0:45)

Keyword search engines provide a somewhat different way to search for information on the Web. Whereas subject indexes like Yahoo and the Librarians' Guide to the Internet arrange Web sites under categories for browsing, search engines allow you to type in words and phrases and search for those anywhere on the Web.

Search engines work by using automated programs that scan the Web; all the sites and their pages are then put in a huge database. So keyword search engines don't include just the titles of Web sites—they can include every word on every page. We are talking about millions and millions of pages.

That means that, while subject indexes are good for browsing, search engines are good for finding esoteric or very specific information. It also means that you can retrieve a lot of irrelevant sites, just because there is so much information on the Web and searching by keywords can be tricky.

Even though search engines include so much, studies have shown that no individual search engine covers the whole Web. So if you can't find what you're looking for the first time, it is a good idea to try more than one. We are going to practice on two of the major search engines today.

ALTAVISTA (*http://altavista.digital.com/*)

Overview (0:45–0:50)

Let's all go to AltaVista now.

> *[Have everyone select the link or type in the address with you.]*

As you may remember, we introduced the AltaVista search engine in the "Getting Started on the World Wide Web" workshop. Let's take a closer look now.

As you can see, AltaVista has some of the same features as Yahoo and many other commercial search services these days: free e-mail, advertisements, some special content areas. Like Yahoo, too, they also provide a subject index of Web resources, here under Browse Categories; let's go ahead and take a quick look at that.

> *[Have everyone select the link.]*

It looks a bit different from Yahoo—all the search services have their own look—but it works basically the same. You click on a category, that takes you to a subcategory, and so forth, until you get to a list of sites.

That can be useful. But what AltaVista is mainly known for is its search engine; let's look at that now. Click back to AltaVista's home page.

[Have everyone click on AltaVista Home.]

Sample Search (0:50–1:00)

[It is crucial to check this sample search (and any other search you are going to demonstrate) in advance, preferably right before class to avoid last-minute surprises.]

What I'd like to do now is a sample search using the AltaVista search engine, and I'd like everyone to do on your computers what I am going to do on mine.

The topic is irises. I'd like to learn how to grow irises in my garden, and I want to search the Web for information on this topic. What we're going to demonstrate is how to refine that search, make it better and more specific, and thereby get better results.

Now the easiest way to search for information about irises is to click in the AltaVista search box at the top and type in the word *iris*. Let's all do that now, and after you've typed in the word you can either use the mouse and click on the Search button, or just hit the Enter key and it will perform the search.

[Allow time for everyone to perform this search.]

Everybody with me? OK, let's look at our results. As we scroll down, it looks like there are a lot of sites that aren't about flowers, and also lots of sites that aren't in English. Let's say we're only interested in English-language sites. It's easy in AltaVista to limit by language. Let's go to the drop-down menu at the top here and select English, and then click Search or hit the Enter key again to perform the search again.

[Allow time for everyone to perform this search.]

Everybody there? We got rid of all the non-English sites, but we've still got all those sites that have nothing to do with flowers. That's because *iris* can refer to lots of things besides flowers: it is a woman's name, it is part of the eye. It looks like it is also used as the name of companies, products, even a computer system.

So let's try to narrow our search. One good way to do that is to add more keywords to the search. Let's click in the box and add the word *flower* to the word *iris*, leaving a space between the two words. AltaVista will then rank highest those sites that have both of those words on their pages, and it will bring those sites to the top of the list. Let's do that search now.

[Allow time for everyone to perform this search.]

Everybody with me? OK, this is looking better. We're mostly getting flower shops, flower societies. These sites might have some good information about growing irises, and you could stop your search here and rummage around those sites a little bit. Or, we can try to add another word and narrow the search even more. Let's add the word *grow* to our search and see what happens. So now our search is *flower iris grow*.

[Allow time for everyone to perform this search.]

AltaVista looks for sites that have any of these words and ranks at the top those sites that have all three. We're still getting a lot of flower shops, though, so I'm going to suggest one other tip. If we put plus signs in front of each word, that means all three words are required to appear, and this can narrow the search even further. Let's try that. Our search is now *+iris +flower +grow*

[Allow time for everyone to perform this search.]

OK, this is looking even better. Here are some sites that are really on target, all about growing irises. Notice that some of the pages are about growing particular types of irises. That would be another good way to narrow your search: if you were interested in a particular kind of iris, it would be a good idea to use that specific name and you would get more targeted results.

There are other ways to narrow searches, and many of them are explained by AltaVista in their Tips page. Let's just take a quick look at that.

[Have everyone select the Tips link.]

This is where you can learn more about good searching techniques. This is where I learned about using the plus sign, for instance. Some other good tips on this page include using quotation marks when searching for a phrase—a very useful technique. Capitalization is also covered. Most of the time you won't want to capitalize your words in AltaVista, because then it will search for both capitalized and lowercase words.

Does anyone have any questions about the search we just performed?

Let's click back to the AltaVista main page.

[Have everyone click back to the AltaVista search page.]

Audience Suggestion (1:00–1:05)

OK, does anyone have a suggestion for something to look for using the AltaVista search engine?

> *[Get a suggestion from the audience. When you receive a suggestion, try to find the answer or the resource using AltaVista, and explain why you are using those particular search methods. (You may have to conduct a quick reference interview with the participant.) Also, consider asking the other participants—or even the person who made the suggestion—how they might go about constructing the search. If you have time, do more than one sample search. Try to make the searches successful, or at least explain why they may not be successful with this resource, and suggest other resources.]*

AltaVista is very flexible and powerful in its searching capabilities, and it has millions of Web pages indexed. The important thing to remember is to narrow your search, using some of the techniques we just learned about.

But no one search engine has it all, and search capabilities differ, so now we're going to turn to another search engine. Are there any questions about AltaVista, before we move on?

HotBot (*http://www.hotbot.com/*)

Overview (1:05–1:10)

Let's all go to HotBot now.

> *[Have everyone select the link or type in the address with you.]*

Like AltaVista and the other search services, HotBot has other features besides its search engine. It, too, has a directory of Web sites to browse. It provides access to online yellow pages and white pages, e-mail addresses, and news stories. Also, because HotBot is affiliated with *Wired* magazine, you will find lots of stories and features about technology.

But, again, HotBot's claim to fame is its search engine, which has received a lot of favorable reviews lately. Let's take a closer look at that.

Sample Search (1:10–1:15)

HotBot has a lot of the same searching capabilities as AltaVista, but it has a different look and operates a little differently. As you can see, there is a search box at the top, just like AltaVista, where you can type in keywords and perform your search. As with AltaVista, because HotBot includes so many millions of Web pages, it is important that you narrow your search and be as specific as possible.

HotBot uses pull-down menus and buttons to help you refine your search. Below the search box, you see a number of different options. The first is a pull-down menu of what to "Look For," with the default being to look for "all the words." This would be similar to using the plus sign in AltaVista. Probably most often you'll want to leave it at this default setting.

The other major options here include searching for (1) "any of the words," which means that at least one of the words has to appear (a broad search); (2) "the exact phrase," which means that the words you type in have to appear in that order (a very useful, narrow search); and (3) "the person," which means that HotBot will search for the name of a person, whether it appears first name first, first name last, etc.

Other pull-down menu options under "Look For" include being able to search by date, by location, and by domain type. For instance, you might want to search only for documents published in the last two weeks, or only for educational institutions, or only for Web sites in South America. If you don't check the boxes next to these menu choices, though, HotBot will not limit by those criteria[*demonstrate checking boxes*]. Most of the time, you probably won't want to limit your searches in that way.

There are also options to limit by type of media included. Again, most of the time you won't want to limit your searches in that way, unless you are looking for something very specific (a picture of a giraffe, for example).

And finally, you have the option of tailoring how you want your searches to display. Let's leave that at the default of ten records at a time, with the long descriptions.

Like AltaVista, HotBot has some help pages (the link is in the upper right corner), which go into greater detail about some of the searching options available. One of the nice things about HotBot, though, is that, because of the menu choices, it is so easy to use right off the bat.

Individual Searches (1:15–1:20)

Now, take about five minutes and you can do some searching in HotBot on your own. Feel free to explore any of its searching features, even ones we didn't go over. Search for whatever you are interested in, and I'll be walking around if you need any assistance.

[Individual searching time. Circulate and provide assistance as necessary.]

Other Methods

OTHER SEARCH ENGINES (1:20–1:22)

We have covered a number of search options and services today, but I want to emphasize that there are many other options when searching for information on the Web.

For one thing, a number of different search engines and directories are available, in addition to the ones we covered today. I have listed these on the handouts that you will take with you today [*pages 84–88*]. All of the search engines are a little bit different, and many include both a subject directory of sites and a keyword search engine. I showed you some of my favorites today, and some sites that are consistently highly rated by reviewers, but you might want to check out these others, as well.

STARTING WITH A SITE YOU KNOW (1:22–1:25)

Another excellent method for finding information on the Web is to start with a major organization or agency in the subject area that interests you. In addition to providing information, very often its Web site will provide good links to other sites in that subject area. For instance, if you want to learn more about cancer, a good place to start might be the National Cancer Institute. And you could easily find its URL through Yahoo, or one of the other search engines, or a print directory like the *Internet Yellow Pages*. So keep this technique in mind, also, when searching for information.

Review (1:25–1:30)

We covered a lot of material today. Let's do a quick recap.

We learned about two major types of search services: subject directories and keyword search engines.

Subject directories categorize Internet resources under subject headings. They are really good for browsing and for starting a search. We went over two different subject directories: the Librarians' Index to the Internet, which is selective and focuses on reference-oriented sites, and Yahoo, which is less selective and is good for finding commercial and individual sites.

Search engines allow you to search by key words and phrases, and they allow you to modify your searching in different ways. They include millions of pages, and are therefore good at finding more obscure or specific things. But because they include so much, it is important to narrow your search and make it as specific as possible. We covered two major search engines—AltaVista and HotBot—and went over ways to refine searches in each.

Thank you all for coming today. The best way to keep learning these search services and techniques is to continue to use them. When you are using the Internet at the library, if you ever have questions about how to use a search engine or construct a search, please don't hesitate to ask me or one of the other staff members here; we'll be happy to help. Thanks!

USING SEARCH ENGINES AND FINDING INFORMATION ON THE WEB AGENDA

Introduction

Welcome
Prerequisites
Objectives

Subject Directories

- Introduction
- Librarians' Index to the Internet (*http://sunsite.berkeley.edu/InternetIndex/*)
  1. Overview
  2. Sample Search
  3. Audience Suggestion
- Yahoo (*http://www.yahoo.com/*)
  1. Overview
  2. Sample Search
  3. Individual Searches

Search Engines

- Introduction
- AltaVista (*http://altavista.digital.com/*)
  1. Overview
  2. Sample Search
  3. Audience Suggestion
- HotBot (*http://www.hotbot.com/*)
  1. Overview
  2. Sample Search
  3. Individual Searches

Other Methods

- Other Search Engines
- Starting with a Site You Know

Review

USING SEARCH ENGINES AND FINDING INFORMATION

KEY POINTS

Subject Directories arrange World Wide Web resources under subject headings. They are useful for browsing to see what sites are available related to a subject category. They vary in how selective they are and in whether they evaluate the resources included. Two examples of subject directories are the Librarians' Index to the Internet (*http://sunsite.berkeley.edu/InternetIndex/*), which is selective and focuses on reference-oriented sites, and Yahoo (*http://www.yahoo.com/*), which is less selective and includes more commercial sites.

Search Engines allow you to search the Web by typing in key words and phrases. They utilize automated robots to include millions of Web pages in their databases. Search engines are therefore good at finding obscure and specific information. It is useful to be as targeted as possible in your search. Each search engine looks and operates somewhat differently, and each has a "help" or "tips" page that can help you construct a good search. Two major search engines are AltaVista (*http://altavista.digital.com/*) and HotBot (*http://www.hotbot.com/*).

Another good method of finding sites on a particular topic is to start with the Web site of a major institution related to that topic. Often, that institution will maintain a directory of related Web resources, and your search can branch out from there.

USING SEARCH ENGINES AND FINDING INFORMATION

Web Sites

The Web sites below are from the training session. A few other useful sites have been added.

Librarians' Index to the Internet

http://sunsite.berkeley.edu/InternetIndex/

An annotated subject directory of evaluated, reference-oriented sites.

Yahoo

http://www.yahoo.com/

A subject index. Also offers news, e-mail, classified ads, regional guides, and other services.

AltaVista

http://altavista.digital.com/

A keyword search engine. Also includes a subject directory and other features.

HotBot

http://www.hotbot.com/

Uses drop-down menus and buttons to allow users to customize Web searches.

Excite

http://www.excite.com/

Offers a keyword search engine, subject searches, news, and personalization options.

Infoseek

http://www.infoseek.com/

Includes both a keyword search engine and subject "channels" for browsing.

Lycos

http://www.lycos.com/

Another search service that offers both keyword searches and subject "guides."

Snap

http://www.snap.com/

Mainly a subject directory. Also includes a complete Web search and other features.

The Mining Company

http://home.miningco.com/

Includes annotated guides to Internet resources on a variety of topics.

Magellan Internet Guide

http://www.mckinley.com/

Includes reviews of Web sites and "green light" sites for children.

Search.com

http://www.search.com/

Includes specialized search engines arranged by topic.

DejaNews

http://www.dejanews.com/

A search engine for Internet discussion groups.

The Internet Sleuth

http://www.isleuth.com/

Includes thousands of searchable databases, many of them missed by other engines.

MetaCrawler

http://www.metacrawler.com/

Queries a number of search engines at once.

The Argus Clearinghouse

http://www.clearinghouse.net/

A collection of topical guides to Internet resources.

INFOMINE: Scholarly Internet Resource Collections

http://lib-www.ucr.edu/

A subject directory that focuses on academic resources.

FURTHER READING AND RESOURCES

Listed below are just a few of the many available Web sites and books about searching the World Wide Web. Please consult the library's catalog or ask a librarian for more recommendations.

Books

Glossbrenner, Alfred, and Emily Glossbrenner. *Search Engines for the World Wide Web: Visual Quickstart Guide.* Berkeley, Calif.: Peachpit Press, 1997.

Presents an introduction to major Web search engines.

Hill, Brad. *World Wide Web Searching for Dummies.* Foster City, Calif.: IDG Books Worldwide, 1997.

Explains the fundamentals of Web searching techniques.

Maze, Susan, et al. *Authoritative Guide to Web Search Engines.* New York: Neal-Schuman Publishers, 1997.

Includes charts that compare features of popular search engines.

Pfanneberger, Bryan. *Web Search Strategies.* Foster City, Calif.: IDG Books, 1996.

Offers a seven-step strategy for finding information on the Web.

Sonnenreich, Wes, and Tim MacInta. *Web Developer.Com Guide to Search Engines.* New York: John Wiley, 1998.

Serves as a guide to search engines for users as well as Web developers.

Web Sites

Search Engine Watch

http://www.searchenginewatch.com/

Includes background information on search engines and tips on how to use them better.

USING SEARCH ENGINES AND FINDING INFORMATION—(CONTINUED)

Search Insider

http://www.searchinsider.com/

Provides tips, tutorials, and feature articles on searching the Web for information.

Search Engines Showdown

http://imt.net/~notess/search/index.html

Features comparison charts and reviews of various search services.

Search Engines (WebReference.com)

http://webreference.com/content/search/

Provides an explanation of how search engines work and how to use them effectively.

Searching the Internet: Recommended Sites and Search Techniques

http://www.albany.edu/library/internet/search.html

Presents an overview of strengths and weaknesses of major search engines and directories.

Literature about Search Services

http://www.ub2.lu.se//desire/radar/lit-about-search-services.html

Lists print and online articles about search engines.

Crawling the Web

http://www.zdnet.com/pcmag/issues/1513/pcmg0045.htm

Offers a technical explanation of how automated robots and search engines work.

Scout Toolkit

http://wwwscout.cs.wisc.edu/scout/toolkit/

Includes reviews of subject guides to the Web, search engines, and online Internet publications.

6
Books and Literature on the Web

Handouts for this workshop follow page 105.

OVERVIEW

Who

The prerequisite for this workshop is the "Getting Started on the World Wide Web" workshop. You may choose to open this workshop to adults who have not taken that workshop, but they must already have a basic understanding of how to navigate the Web, and they must have basic mouse and keyboard abilities. It is recommended that trainees also have taken the "Using Search Engines and Finding Information" workshop prior to this class. While designed for adult patrons of a public library, the following workshop can be adapted easily for any group interested in book and literature information on the Web.

This is a sample workshop for literature enthusiasts. Similar workshops can be created around any number of topics, hobbies, current events, and interests. Choose topics that will be of interest to your clientele!

What

This customizable, ready-to-run workshop is an example of a hands-on, single-subject, Internet training module. It emphasizes activities and interaction to enhance the learning experience. It is a basic introduction to book and literature information on the Web, with an emphasis on current and popular fiction.

Where

This workshop is designed for a computer lab where the students can get hands-on experience searching for information and using the resources. However, the lesson plan can also be used for a lecture or demonstration.

When

This workshop lasts for an hour and a half. Because it is hands-on and includes activities, the time will go quickly.

Why

The objectives of this workshop are for the trainees to be able to (1) explain the various types of book and literature information resources on the Web; (2) effectively utilize specific resources of each type; and (3) apply their understanding to the learning and use of new book and literature information resources, particularly those on the handouts (pages 106–111) for this session.

With a hands-on workshop, the objective is to get the trainees using the computers and the resources. Don't lecture or demonstrate too much; the trainees will learn more when they are doing it themselves. They will also feel frustrated if they have computers in front of them but have to listen to the trainer; if you lecture too much, you may lose them and they may start searching around on their own. Instead, alternate mini-lectures with a variety of activities (such as group games and individual searching).

WORKSHOP AGENDA

This agenda works in conjunction with the handouts (pages 106–111), and the handout should be used throughout the workshop. The agenda follows a very general progression from current literature sites to sites with information on literature of the past. It alternates lecture with activity, group work with individual searching. Since this is a hands-on class, it would help (although it's not necessary) to have an assistant, who can aid anyone who gets stuck and falls behind.

INTRODUCTION

Welcome (0:00–0:01)
Prerequisites (0:01–0:03)
Objectives (0:03–0:05)

BOOKSTORES

Introduction (Amazon.com) (0:05–0:12)
Amazon.com versus Barnes & Noble (0:12–0:16)
Other Online Bookstores (0:16–0:18)
Book Industry and Publisher Sites (0:18–0:20)

AUTHORS

Authors on the Highway (0:20–0:27)
Other Author Information Resources (0:27–0:30)

BOOK REVIEWS

The New York Times: Books (0:30–0:37)
NY Times: Individual Searching: (0:37–0:42)
Other Book Review Resources (0:42–0:45)

GENRE FICTION

Introduction (0:45–0:48)
Individual Searches on Favorite Genre (0:48–0:55)

FULL TEXT

Introduction (0:55–0:58)
IPL Online Texts Collection: Dickens and Dickinson (0:58–1:05)
Other Online Text Collections (1:05–1:07)

BOOK AWARDS

Introduction (1:07–1:10)
Searching Game (1:10–1:17)

LIBRARIES

Introduction (1:17–1:20)
Home (1:20–1:27)

REVIEW (1:27–1:30)

SAMPLE SCRIPT

This session is very hands-on. It is important, therefore, that everyone have taken the "Getting Started on the World Wide Web" workshop and/or be competent in basic computer and Web navigation skills. Be clear about when the trainees should work on their machines, and when they should just watch and listen to you.

Also, be aware that Web site design invariably changes over time. Be sure to review any parts of this script that refer to specific aspects of a site's layout or navigation, and make any necessary updates.

This will be a fun session; you will have an audience who loves books and will be very interested in the content of this workshop.

Introduction

WELCOME (0:00–0:01)

Hello! Welcome to the "Books and Literature on the Web" workshop. The Web is a great place for those of us who love books; there is an amazing amount of fun and useful information about books on the Web, and we're going to tap into some of that today.

PREREQUISITES (0:01–0:03)

Everyone here should already have taken the "Getting Started on the World Wide Web" workshop. If you haven't taken that workshop, for this session you need to have a basic understanding of the Internet and how to navigate the Web. Everybody must also have basic mouse and keyboard skills, since this is going to be a hands-on class. Is anyone in the wrong place, or does anybody have any questions about that?

OBJECTIVES (0:03–0:05)

OK, we have three main objectives for this workshop.

> *[Have the three objectives already written on the board or flip chart, and reveal them at this time.]*

At the end of this hour and a half, we will be able to (1) explain the various types of book and literature information resources on the Web; (2) effectively use specific resources of each type; and (3) apply this understanding to the learning and use of new book and literature information resources, particularly those on the handouts (pages 106–111) for this session. Did everybody get the handouts?

And, as I said, this is going to be a hands-on class, with lots of searching and activity. We are really going to use these resources. So let's get started!

Bookstores

INTRODUCTION (AMAZON.COM) (0:05–0:12)

Let's start with crass commercialism. Of course, there are lots of things you can buy online these days—just about anything you can buy in a store you can also buy online. And this is true of books. In fact, one of the truly successful areas of Internet commerce has been the selling of books, and the first major venture was a company called Amazon.com (*http://www.amazon.com/*). You may already be familiar with it. Let's go to their Web site now.

[Have everyone click on the link or type in the address with you.]

Unlike some other bookstore Web sites we are going to talk about, like Barnes and Noble (*http://www.barnesandnoble.com/*) and Borders (*http://www.borders.com/*), Amazon.com only exists on the Internet; there is no physical retail store where you can go and shop. Amazon would say that this allows them to have lower prices because they don't have the cost of keeping retail shelves stocked with books; they just need a distribution center. We'll compare prices in a few minutes.

Other than the fact that they only exist online, however, Amazon is pretty similar to other online bookstores. Let's take a closer look. Everybody there?

Amazon.com allows you to search for and buy millions of books online, both in print and out-of-print. They also sell music CDs; notice here at the top you can choose books or music. The default is books and we'll stick with that today, but just remember that pretty much everything we'll be doing with books can also be done with music.

You'll also notice on the first page that you can do a keyword search for a book in this box; that search box remains on every page of Amazon so that you can always do a basic search for a book. There is also this navigation bar at the top; it appears on every page and allows you to search for different things. The first option is to do a Book Search, and this has some more searching options than the basic keyword search. Let's choose that now.

[Have everyone select the link.]

Everybody there? Searching is easy on Amazon. As you can see, you can do an author search, a title search, and a subject search. Let's all do a basic author search now. Say I am interested in books by the novelist John Irving. The easiest thing is to do a Last Name, First Name author search and type in *Irving, John*. Let's all type that in now, and then click Search or hit the Enter key.

[Have everyone perform the search.]

And here we have a list of John Irving's books available from Amazon. The list gives us basic information: title, whether it is hardcover or paperback or audio, publication year, price, and shipping information. As you can see, Amazon offers 20 percent to 40 percent discounts on many books, and no sales tax is charged except in the state of Washington. They also offer a variety of shipping options. Standard shipping takes three to seven days, but for an additional fee you can get two-day or next-day air shipping.

If you click on a title, that will usually provide more information about the book. Let's scroll down until we get to the hardcover version of Irving's recent book *A Widow for One Year*, and let's all click on that title.

[Have everyone select the link. Feel free to update the example search with any current popular author or novel.]

Everybody there? So this is what a book page from Amazon often looks like. There is a picture of the cover, pricing and shipping information, a review and synopsis from Amazon, excerpts from other reviews, and customer comments. There is sometimes even an excerpt from the book. And there is the button Add to Shopping Cart. You would choose this if you want to purchase this book, or think you might want to. Amazon allows you to review what is in your shopping cart before making the purchase. When you do decide to buy, you type in your credit card number, or they also allow you to call in your card number if you wish. When you order online, though, your information is encrypted; in other words, it is scrambled when it is sent, so there is really no security concern when sending your credit card number to them over the Internet. I would worry more about someone overhearing me say my card number on the phone!

So that's really all there is to it to search for and buy books online at Amazon. You don't get the social aspect of going to a bookstore, and you can't pick up the books and look through them, but it can be a convenient and cost-effective way to shop. We're going to do a little comparison shopping in a minute, but first I want to quickly go over the other resources that Amazon offers. These are available under the various options along the navigation bar at the top.

Next to the Book Search button on the navigation bar is the Browse Subjects option. This function allows you to see lists of Amazon's top sellers arranged by subject. Next to that, Bestsellers lists Amazon's bestsellers for fiction and nonfiction, paperback and hardcover. Featured in the Media highlights books that have been reviewed in various newspapers, magazines, and radio programs. Award Winners lists winners of many different book awards; remember this later when we return to book awards. The Gift Center includes gift ideas and gift certificates. Kids offers book recommendations and bestseller lists for children and teenagers. And the Recommendation Center offers various recommended reading resources; for example, you can tell them what you like to read, and they will offer recommendations of books you might like. So Amazon offers a lot more than just low prices on books.

AMAZON.COM VERSUS BARNES & NOBLE (0:12–0:16)

[Next, divide the group in half. One half will be the Amazon group, and the other half will be the Barnes & Noble group. Give them a book to search for, and then ask what prices they found and compare. This should be a quick, fun activity which will get the whole group involved.

You may have time to do two or three books. Pick different types of books—say, a current bestseller, a standard hardcover or paperback (for example, Toni Morrison's novel Sula), and an out-of-print book (for example, Angel Fire, by Joyce Carol Oates). Including the out-of-print option will allow you to explain how Amazon will search for out-of-print books and provide notification via e-mail; Barnes & Noble does not currently provide this service and does not include out-of-print books in their database.]

OTHER ONLINE BOOKSTORES (0:16–0:18)

Besides Amazon.com and Barnes & Noble, there are many, many other bookstores on the Internet—chains and independents, general and specialty. If everyone would refer to your handouts for a minute, you'll see some of them listed there.

Borders, another bookstore chain we have already mentioned, also has a Web site, which includes books, music, and videos.

Another useful site is from Germany and is called Acses (*http://www.acses.com/*). This site simultaneously searches a number of online bookstores (including Amazon and Barnes & Noble) and compares prices. We could have used this one! Because it searches a number of sites at once, however, it can sometimes be slow.

And then there are some sites for out-of-print, rare, and antiquarian books:

Bibliofind (*http://www.bibliofind.com/*), Interloc (*http://www.interloc.com/*), and Advanced Book Exchange (*http://www.abebooks.com/*). These are terrific sites if you are a book collector, or if you are interested in that area.

Finally, the BookWire Index to Booksellers (*http://www.bookwire.com/index/booksellers.html*) is a good directory of online bookstores. Here you can find links to the Web sites of lots of independent and specialty bookstores throughout the country.

BOOK INDUSTRY AND PUBLISHER SITES (0:18–0:20)

If we continue down the list of sites on our handout, the home page for BookWire (*http://www.bookwire.com/*) is listed. This is mainly a book industry site—for instance, it has industry news from *Publishers Weekly*. But it also has a lot of great information for consumers—like that index to booksellers I mentioned above—and we are going to return to various sub-pages on BookWire throughout the session today.

Another really useful book industry site is the American Booksellers Association's BookWeb (*http://ambook.org/*). One of the great things about this site is its directory of independent bookstores, just in case you want to find a physical (not virtual) bookstore in your neighborhood.

Then, if you continue down the handout, you will see some resources for publishers and publishers' catalogs. Almost every publisher maintains a Web site these days—certainly all the major ones do—and they will usually have an online catalog of their titles along with the option to order their books online. They also often have biographical and other information about their authors, and other resources depending on their specialty. They can be great sites, and I encourage you to explore them on your own.

Authors

AUTHORS ON THE HIGHWAY (0:20–0:27)

Publishers often like to give information about their authors. They also like to send them on tours to give readings and signings to promote their books. One section of the BookWire site provides a calendar of author appearances throughout the country. It's called Authors on the Highway (*http://www.bookwire.com/highway/*). Let's go there now.

[Have everyone click on the link or type in the address with you.]

BookWire's list is by no means complete, but it's pretty extensive and is a great way of keeping track of where a particular author is appearing, or who is appearing in a particular city. Unfortunately, it doesn't include author appearances at libraries, but we will return to libraries at the end of today's session. As you can see, we can search by author, title, publisher, state, city, even bookstore. Let's do a search together.

[Lead them through a local search by city (or, if more appropriate, by state), down to the bookstore level. After this, let them do a few minutes of individual searching for authors or areas they are interested in.]

OTHER AUTHOR INFORMATION RESOURCES (0:27–0:30)

We have mentioned that you can often get author information from publisher sites, and we have just learned about author appearances. But there is a lot more author information available on the Web. Authors often have entire Web sites devoted to them. These can be publisher sites, as we mentioned, or they can be pages from colleges and universities where they teach. Or they can be academic studies of a particular author. Often, they are individual fan pages. Many of these can be found through a directory, such as Yahoo, which you all know about. Your handouts [*pages 106–111*] list a few other good starting points for author information.

American Authors on the Web (*http://ernie.lang.nagoya-u.ac.jp/~matsuoka/ AmeLit.html*) and British and Irish Authors on the Web (*http:// ernie.lang.nagoya-u.ac.jp/~matsuoka/UK-authors.html*) are chronologically arranged lists of links to information about past and contemporary authors. The Online Literary Criticism Collection site (*http://www.ipl.org/ref/litcrit/*) from the Internet Public Library is an excellent resource that provides annotated links to critical and biographical sites for American and British authors; it tends to focus on academic and scholarly resources. And A Celebration of Women Writers (*http://www.cs.cmu.edu/People/mmbt/women/writers.html*) is another excellent resource for links to biographical and bibliographic information about women writers; it also includes links to the full text of many of these writers' works.

Book Reviews

THE NEW YORK TIMES: BOOKS (0:30–0:37)

We have learned about buying books online and about finding author information, including author tours, online. But what if you want some guidance on what books to read? Well, we saw that Amazon has a lot of review excerpts and other recommended reading tools, and the library also has a lot of readers' advisory resources, as well. You can also go straight to many review sources online. For instance, The New York Times: Books (*http://www.nytimes.com/ books/*) offers an extensive archive of reviews, and more. Let's all go there now.

[Have everyone click on the link or type in the address with you.]

Everybody there? Let's look around this introductory page of The New York Times: Books; we will be able to see a lot of what is offered, in addition to reviews. Along the left are some of the main contents of the site. You'll notice that you can read the contents of this Sunday's Book Review section, and there are also some daily updates. There is also a section on Expanded Bestsellers; these are longer lists than you will find in the print edition. There is also a section called First Chapters; let's all click on that.

[Have everyone select the link.]

Here, the *New York Times* provides the full text of first chapters of a number of recent novels and other books. They highlight some current books, and you can also browse by author. Let's choose Fiction.

[Have everyone select the link.]

So, you see, it's quite a healthy selection of first chapters. This can be a fun way to browse and decide whether you want to read an entire book or not; it's like browsing in the bookstore or the library.

Now, let's click back until we get to that Contents listing again.

[Have everyone click back to a page with the Contents listing.]

There is a section for special features that includes some audio clips of authors. And there are discussion forums on a variety of topics, including particular authors. This can be a fun way to share your thoughts and read the opinions of others; I encourage you to explore them on your own.

But the heart of this site is the archive of reviews. The *New York Times* offers an archive of their reviews back to 1980—tens of thousands of reviews. Let's all do one search together; let's look for that John Irving book again—*A Widow for One Year*. We can either search by author or by title. If we put the name or title in quotation marks, it will search for the words as a phrase. I suggest we search for the title this way: "widow for one year." Let's all do that now.

[Have everyone perform the search.]

And, you see, that got us our review right away.

NY Times: Individual Searching: (0:37–0:42)

Let's take a few minutes and do a little individual searching on The New York Times: Books. Look for a review of a book you recently read, or one you are thinking about reading. Or explore the discussion forums a little bit. I'll wander around and be available to help out if you need me.

[Individual Searching.]

Other Book Review Resources (0:42–0:45)

In addition to The New York Times: Books, there are many other book review sources on the Web, both professional and informal, and some of these are listed on your handout.

The New York Review of Books (*http://www.nybooks.com/nyrev/index.html*) offers selections from its reviews, and the online version of the *Washington Post* (*http://www.washingtonpost.com/wp-srv/style/books/front.htm*) includes reviews, first chapters, and bestseller lists. BookWire (*http://www.bookwire.com/reviews/*), which we have already talked about, offers reviews from a number of sources, including *Library Journal, Hungry Mind Review, Boston Book Review*, and more. *Booklist*, which is a print publication, has an online counterpart (*http://www.ala.org/booklist/index.html*) that provides brief reviews on a wide range of new books, both fiction and nonfiction. And, finally, if you need more, AcqWeb's Directory of Book Reviews on the Web (*http://www.library.vanderbilt.edu/law/acqs/bookrev.html*) provides an extensive directory of book review sites on the Web.

Genre Fiction

Introduction (0:45–0:48)

Moving down to the next section on your handout, we are going to turn to sites about what some people call genre fiction. These are novels and stories of specific types or genres, such as mysteries or science fiction. I bet most of you, being book lovers, have a favorite genre or two.

The Web has a lot of information on genre fiction, both professional sites as well as private sites maintained by enthusiasts. These can have author information, reviews, recommended reading lists, discussion forums, and other information. What we are going to do, since you all probably like different genres, is some individual searching on these sites; you can explore whatever site or sites look interesting to you.

Looking at your handout, The Mysterious Home Page (*http://www.webfic.com/mysthome/*) offers a great guide to Internet resources on mysteries and crime fiction. For science fiction lovers, SF Site (*http://www.sfsite.com/*) has reviews, features, and a comprehensive list of links to author Web sites, while the Internet Speculative Fiction DataBase (*http://www.sfsite.com/isfdb/*) provides a catalog of works of science fiction, fantasy, and horror, including forthcoming books. For romance novel enthusiasts, The Romance Reader (*http://www.theromancereader.com/*) includes reviews of various types of romance novels, plus other features. Stephen King fans will like the Horror in Literature site (*http://www.drcasey.com/literature/index.shtml*), which offers bibliographies, links to author pages, and other features. Soon's Historical Fiction Site (*http://uts.cc.utexas.edu/~soon/histfiction/index.html*) provides author information, bibliographies, answers to frequently asked questions, and more. If we have any Louis L'Amour fans, you might want to turn to Jim Janke's Old West (*http://homepages.dsu.edu/jankej/oldwest/oldwest.htm*) and look in the section Novels, Novelists, and Short Fiction. Finally, if you really can't decide, you might want to go to BookBrowser: A Guide for Avid Readers (*http://www.bookbrowser.com/*), which includes recommended fiction reading lists in a variety of genres; it also has more general reading lists, if you are really not a fan of any of these particular genres.

INDIVIDUAL SEARCHES ON FAVORITE GENRE (0:48–0:55)

Let's take about seven minutes and look at some of these sites. Go to whichever one you want, and I'll wander around and be available to answer any questions. Have fun!

[Individual searching.]

Full Text

INTRODUCTION (0:55–0:58)

For a while now, various sites on the Internet have offered the full text of classic works of literature. So you can get an entire nineteenth-century scientific treatise online, for instance, or an entire eighteenth-century novel, or the complete works of Chaucer. What is available for free online has tended to be older works, from the beginning part of this century and earlier. Why do you think that is?

[Get responses.]

It's because of copyright restriction that newer works are not posted online for free, or at least not legally. That's also why, for instance, the *New York*

Times can only post a portion (the first chapters) of recent works. But the copyright has expired on these older works, so they can be published online, distributed, and reproduced. And it's amazing what you can find.

IPL ONLINE TEXTS COLLECTION: DICKENS AND DICKINSON (0:58–1:05)

Let's go to a site that is a great jumping-off point for online texts. It's from the Internet Public Library and it's called the IPL Online Texts Collection (*http://www.ipl.org/reading/books/*). Let's all go there now.

[Have everyone click on the link or type in the address with you.]

This site basically provides a catalog and links for thousands of titles that are available in full text on the Internet. You can browse the site by author, title, and Dewey Classification, just as in a library; you can also do a keyword search. Let's say I want to see what works by Charles Dickens are available on the Internet; I can simply select to browse authors beginning with *D*. Let's all do that now.

[Have everyone select the link.]

After the page finishes loading, we can scroll down until we come to works by Charles Dickens. And you'll see that there are quite a few. You can click on the title, and that will take you directly to the full text of that work on the site that makes it available. Some titles are listed more than once; that means that more than one site has made that work available. Works can be provided in various formats, so you may want to explore more than one site. If you click on Full Entry you will get more information about the title, including where it is located. Let's all click on the Full Entry for the first version of *Great Expectations*.

[Have everyone select the link. Be sure to preview this search in advance to ensure that search results have not changed since this book's publication.]

This provides us with other searching options, and also tells us that this title is made available from the University of Virginia Electronic Text Library. Let's all click on the URL and go there now.

[Have everyone select the link.]

Now we've gone to the site with the work itself. It's probably still loading— that's because this is a long novel! Many hundreds of pages, as I recall. You can scroll down, and see some preliminary matter and then the beginning of the work itself.

Now, I don't know about you, but I have a hard time imagining that I am going to want to read this entire long novel on the computer. And I usually don't like to curl up in bed with a computer! I think I'd rather read the paperback. Still, having this available can be useful if you want to read selections; also, many works that you may have a hard time finding anywhere else are available on the Internet. And there is a lot of work being done on hand-held computer devices and computer screens with better resolutions. So the day may come fairly soon when you will be able to read comfortably an entire book online.

In the meantime, though, I'll stick to shorter works. Let's all click back until we get back to the Internet Public Library and its list of authors beginning with D.

[Have everyone click back to IPL's listing of authors beginning with D.]

Everybody there? If we scroll down, right under Dickens comes the poet Emily Dickinson. Let's try Selected Poems.

[Have everyone select the link.]

Here we have selected poems by Dickinson, in alphabetical order. Let's try one—the poem that begins "I'm nobody."

[Have everyone select the link.]

And here is this famous poem by Emily Dickinson. Eight lines—*that* I can handle reading online!

Other Online Text Collections (1:05–1:07)

The Online Texts Collection at the Internet Public Library is a great starting point, but there are other terrific online text resources on the Web, and some of these are listed on your handout.

The On-Line Books Page (*http://www.cs.cmu.edu/books.html*) is similar to the Internet Public Library's site; it also provides a searchable index of thousands of online books and other works. The English Server (*http://eserver.org/*) includes both fiction and nonfiction works on its site. A really interesting specialized site is called Classic Short Stories (*http://www.bnl.com/shorts/*); it offers a growing collection of classic short stories online. These are more manageable to read online than an entire Dickens novel! And another great specialized site is The Complete Works of William Shakespeare (*http://the-tech.mit.edu/Shakespeare/works.html*) from MIT, which includes all the bard's plays and poems, plus famous quotations and a glossary.

Book Awards

INTRODUCTION (1:07–1:10)

Now let's turn our attention to book awards and information online about them. Lots of folks like to read award-winning books, and the Web provides comprehensive lists, along with background information. Many awards sites are listed on your handout.

The Pulitzer Prize site (*http://www.pulitzer.org/*), the National Book Awards (*http://www.bookwire.com/nbf/docs/awards.html*), and The Nobel Prize (*http://www.nobel.se/*) all provide lists of winners past and present. The Children's Literature Web Guide (*http://www.acs.ucalgary.ca/~dkbrown/*), a terrific source for information about literature for children, includes information on Newbery and Caldecott winners. Finally, BookWire (*http://www.bookwire.com/index/book-awards.html*) and Virtual WordsWorth (*http://www.wordsworth.com/*), another online bookstore, maintain extensive awards pages; they include lesser-known awards and awards for genre fiction, for instance. And don't forget that Amazon and Barnes & Noble maintain extensive award lists, too.

SEARCHING GAME (1:10–1:17)

[At this point, play a short trivia game involving book awards. Divide the group into two teams. One at a time, give each team a different question to answer, and do a total of three questions each. A groups gets a point when someone from their team shouts out the correct answer first. Have a "prize"—such as a library bookmark—for each member of the winning team. But also give the "losing" team prizes, and make the prizes things that everyone can pick up for free anyway. Here are a few suggested pairings:

Team A	**Team B**
1. Q: Who won the 1983 Pulitzer Prize for fiction?	Q: Who won the 1983 National Book Award for best first novel?
A: Alice Walker, *The Color Purple*	A: Gloria Naylor, *The Women of Brewster Place*
2. Q: Who won the 1925 Nobel Prize in Literature?	Q: Who won the 1954 Nobel Prize in Literature?
A: George Bernard Shaw	A: Ernest Hemingway

3. Q: Who won the 1985 Hugo
   Award for best science fiction novel?
   A: William Gibson, *Neuromancer*

Q: Who won the 1997 Bram Stoker
   Award for best horror novel?
A: Stephen King, *The Green Mile*.]

Libraries

INTRODUCTION (1:17–1:20)

The final area I want to cover for book and literature information is, you guessed it, the library. Libraries of all types—public, academic, corporate—were some of the first institutions to get on the Internet and make great use of it. Now, you can search the catalogs of libraries around the corner and around the world, and libraries are putting lots of other information and resources on their Web sites, including book lists and digitized collections.

Some libraries and library resources are listed on your handout. The first three—Libweb (*http://sunsite.berkeley.edu/Libweb/*), SJCPL's Public Libraries with WWW Services (*http://sjcpl.lib.in.us/homepage/PublicLibraries/ PublicLibraryServers.html*), and webCATS: Library Catalogues on the World Wide Web (*http://www.lights.com/webcats/*)—provide links to library catalogs and Web sites throughout the country and the world.

HOME (1:20–1:27)

One of these is our library right here.

> [At this point, have everyone go to your library's home page, if it is available, or to the online catalog. Demonstrate the resources that are provided, and offer referrals to workshops and handouts, where more in-depth information can be found.]

Review (1:27–1:30)

We have covered a lot of ground today! Let's just recap quickly.

We have learned about various types of book and literature information available on the Web, and we have looked at specific resources of each type.

We learned about online bookstores, and did a little comparison shopping between Amazon.com and Barnes & Noble.

We talked about author information on the Web, and learned that we can find information about contemporary and past authors. We looked at the Authors on the Highway site, where we could find author tour information.

We explored some sources for book reviews on the Web, and looked specifically at the *New York Times* site, which offers its book reviews and more.

We covered genre fiction: mysteries, science fiction, romance, horror, historical fiction, westerns. We discovered there are sites for all genres.

We did some exploration of full-text sites on the Web, which are widespread and where you can get the entire text of older works. We looked at the Internet Public Library's Online Texts Collection as an excellent directory of texts available on the Web.

We discovered a lot of sites with information on book awards; these can be great resources for selecting what to read.

And finally, we returned to the library. You can search library Web sites and catalogs for book information around the world, and that includes our own library right here.

All of these resources and more are listed on your handout. Please be sure you have one to take with you, and never hesitate to ask us for book information both on the Web and off. Thanks for coming today!

BOOKS AND LITERATURE ON THE WEB AGENDA

Introduction

- Welcome
- Prerequisites
- Objectives

Bookstores

- Introduction (Amazon.com)
- Amazon.com versus Barnes & Noble
- Other Online Bookstores
- Book Industry and Publisher Sites

Authors

- Authors on the Highway
- Other Author Information Resources

Book Reviews

- The New York Times: Books
- NY Times: Individual Searching
- Other Book Review Resources

Genre Fiction

- Introduction
- Individual Searches on Favorite Genre

Full Text

- Introduction
- IPL Online Texts Collection: Dickens and Dickinson
- Other Online Text Collections

Book Awards

- Introduction
- Searching Game

Libraries

- Introduction
- Home

Review

BOOKS AND LITERATURE ON THE WEB: USEFUL SITES

The following are Web sites covered in this training session . . . and a few other useful sites. They follow the order of the workshop.

Bookstores

Amazon.com
> *http://www.amazon.com/*
> A large bookstore available only online. Includes both in-print and out-of-print books.

Barnes & Noble
> *http://www.barnesandnoble.com/*
> The chain's online counterpart. Like Amazon, offers a number of discounts.

Borders.com
> *http://www.borders.com/*
> This chain's online counterpart. Includes books, music, and videos.

Acses
> *http://www.acses.com/*
> Simultaneously searches a number of online bookstores and compares prices.

Bibliofind
> *http://www.bibliofind.com/*
> Millions of old, used, and rare books from booksellers around the world.

Interloc
> *http://www.interloc.com/*
> A large database of out-of-print and antiquarian books for sale.

Advanced Book Exchange (ABE)
> *http://www.abebooks.com/*
> Another resource for out-of-print, used, rare, and antiquarian books.

The BookWire Index: Booksellers
> *http://www.bookwire.com/index/booksellers.html*
> Bookwire's directory of booksellers on the Web.

Book Industry Sites

BookWire
> *http://www.bookwire.com/*
> Includes industry news from *Publishers Weekly* and other publications, bestseller lists, and more.

BookWeb (American Booksellers Association)
> *http://ambook.org/*
> Includes an extensive independent bookstore directory, information about book fairs, statistics, and other resources.

BOOKS AND LITERATURE ON THE WEB: USEFUL SITES—(CONTINUED)

Publishers

Publishers' Catalogues Home Page
http://www.lights.com/publisher/
Includes links to book publishers throughout the world.

The Association of American University Presses
http://aaup.princeton.edu/
A catalog of titles from dozens of university presses. Includes ordering capability.

Antiquarian Booksellers' Association of America (ABAA)
http://www.abaa-booknet.com/
Offers access to hundreds of member catalogs.

The BookWire Index: Publishers
http://www.bookwire.com/index/publishers.html
An index to publishers of all types on the Web.

Authors

Authors on the Highway
http://www.bookwire.com/highway/
An author tour calendar, searchable by author name, title, publisher, city, and bookstore.

American Authors on the Web
http://ernie.lang.nagoya-u.ac.jp/~matsuoka/AmeLit.html
Chronologically arranged list of links to information about American authors.

British and Irish Authors on the Web
http://ernie.lang.nagoya-u.ac.jp/~matsuoka/UK-authors.html
Chronologically arranged list of links to information about British and Irish authors.

Online Literary Criticism Collection
http://www.ipl.org/ref/litcrit/
Provides annotated links to critical and biographical sites for American and British authors. Part of the Internet Public Library.

A Celebration of Women Writers
http://www.cs.cmu.edu/People/mmbt/women/writers.html
Provides links to biographical and bibliographic information about women writers, plus full-text works.

Book Reviews

The New York Times: Books
http://www.nytimes.com/books/
An extensive archive of reviews, bestseller lists, discussions, first chapters, and more.

The New York Review of Books

http://www.nybooks.com/nyrev/index.html

Selections from this intellectual literary review.

Washingtonpost.com

http://www.washingtonpost.com/wp-srv/style/books/front.htm

Includes reviews, first chapters, bestseller lists, and other resources.

BookWire: Reviews

http://www.bookwire.com/reviews/

Includes reviews from *Library Journal, Hungry Mind Review, Boston Book Review,* and more.

Booklist

http://www.ala.org/booklist/index.html

Brief reviews on a wide range of new books.

AcqWeb's Directory of Book Reviews on the Web

http://www.library.vanderbilt.edu/law/acqs/bookrev.html

An extensive directory of book review sites on the Web.

Genre Fiction

The Mysterious Home Page

http://www.webfic.com/mysthome/

An extensive guide to Internet resources on mysteries and crime fiction.

SF Site: The Home Page for Science Fiction and Fantasy

http://www.sfsite.com/

Includes reviews, features, and a comprehensive list of links to author Web sites.

The Internet Speculative Fiction DataBase

http://www.sfsite.com/isfdb/

A catalog of works of science fiction, fantasy, and horror, including forthcoming books.

The Romance Reader

http://www.theromancereader.com/

Offers reviews of various types of romance novels, plus other features.

Horror in Literature

http://www.drcasey.com/literature/index.shtml

Includes bibliographies, links to author pages, and other features.

Soon's Historical Fiction Site

http://uts.cc.utexas.edu/~soon/histfiction/index.html

Includes author information, bibliographies, answers to frequently asked questions, and more.

Jim Janke's Old West

http://homepages.dsu.edu/jankej/oldwest/oldwest.htm

The section Novels, Novelists, and Short Fiction offers resources on western writers.

BookBrowser: A Guide for Avid Readers

http://www.bookbrowser.com/

Recommended fiction reading lists in a variety of genres.

BOOKS AND LITERATURE ON THE WEB: USEFUL SITES—(CONTINUED)

Full Text

IPL Online Texts Collections
http://www.ipl.org/reading/books/
Another searchable index of online texts.

The On-Line Books Page
http://www.cs.cmu.edu/books.html
Searchable index of thousands of online books and other works.

The English Server
http://eserver.org/
Includes fiction and nonfiction works.

Classic Short Stories
http://www.bnl.com/shorts/
A growing collection of classic short stories online.

The Complete Works of William Shakespeare
http://the-tech.mit.edu/Shakespeare/works.html
Includes all of Shakespeare's plays and poems, plus famous quotations and a glossary.

Book Awards

The Pulitzer Prize
http://www.pulitzer.org/
Profiles of recent winners and a list of past recipients.

The National Book Awards
http://www.bookwire.com/nbf/docs/awards.html
A list of previous winners, plus information about eligibility and judges.

The Nobel Prize
http://www.nobel.se/
The official site of the Nobel Foundation. Offers biographical information for all winners.

The Children's Literature Web Guide
http://www.acs.ucalgary.ca/~dkbrown/
Provides information on Newbery and Caldecott winners, plus much more.

The BookWire Index: Book Awards
http://www.bookwire.com/index/book-awards.html
An extensive list of other book award sites on the Web.

Virtual WordsWorth: The Awards Page
http://www.wordsworth.com/
An extensive awards page. Maintained by the bookseller Wordsworth.

Libraries

Libweb
> *http://sunsite.berkeley.edu/Libweb/*
> An extensive international directory of library Web sites.

SJCPL's Public Libraries with WWW Services
> *http://sjcpl.lib.in.us/homepage/PublicLibraries/PublicLibraryServers.html*
> A comprehensive list of public libraries on the Web.

webCATS: Library Catalogues on the World Wide Web
> *http://www.lights.com/webcats/*
> A list of library catalogs available on the Web.

Library of Congress
> *http://lcweb.loc.gov/*
> Provides access to the Library of Congress catalog, digital collections, exhibitions, and government resources.

The New York Public Library
> *http://www.nypl.org/*
> Includes the catalogs, digital collections, and guides for children and teenagers.

The Internet Public Library
> *http://www.ipl.org/*
> A "virtual" library, with online collections, research guides, and a reference service.

FURTHER READING AND RESOURCES

Books

Morris, Evan. *The Book Lover's Guide to the Internet.* New York: Fawcett, 1996.
> A beginner's guide to literary resources on the Internet.

Web Sites

BookSpot
> *http://www.bookspot.com/*
> A basic guide to book-related resources on the Web.

The World Wide Web Virtual Library: Literature
> *http://sunsite.unc.edu/ibic/guide.html*
> Also known as The IBIC Guide to Book-Related Resources on the Internet.

7

College Information on the Web

Handouts for this workshop
follow page 131.

OVERVIEW

Who

This demonstration is for high school students who are planning to apply to college, and their parents. It should be expected that everyone has taken the "Getting Started on the World Wide Web" workshop and/or has a basic understanding of the Web and how to search it.

What

This customizable, ready-to-run workshop is an example of a demonstration, single-subject Internet training module. This demonstration is an introduction to finding college information on the Web, including college and university Web sites, information on selecting a college, the application process, financial aid information, standardized tests, and information on distance education and adult learning. Its focus is the Web and information resources on the Web. While it is not an overview of the entire college selection and application process, it takes its structure from that process and also points the attendees to additional information resources.

Where

This training is designed as a demonstration for a classroom of trainees (10–30 people). The instructor uses a computer with projection; the attendees do not have computers. The size, then, is really not limited; the demonstration could easily be adapted for a large lecture hall, as well as a smaller group. It could also easily be used as the basis for a hands-on workshop.

When

This demonstration lasts one hour and 15 minutes. It should be offered at times when both high school students and their parents are likely to be available (for example, evenings or weekends).

Why

The objectives of this workshop are for the trainees to be able to (1) explain the various types of college information resources on the Web; (2) use specific resources of each type effectively and incorporate them into the college planning and application process; and (3) apply their knowledge to the learning and use of new college information resources, particularly those on the handouts for this session.

WORKSHOP AGENDA

This agenda works in conjunction with the handout, and the handout should be used and referred to throughout the workshop. There are many substantial areas to cover in this demonstration (for example, financial aid, the decision-making process), so for each general topic it alternates between general points and a demonstration of one or two specific sites. You may want to allow some time after the demonstration for answering individual questions.

INTRODUCTION

Welcome (0:00–0:01)
Prerequisites (0:01–0:02)
Objectives (0:02–0:05)

COLLEGES AND UNIVERSITIES

Introduction (0:05–0:08)
Yahoo Search (0:08–0:13)
Sample College Web Site (0:13–0:20)
Other College and University Sites (0:20–0:23)

PLANNING, DECIDING, AND APPLYING

Overview (College Choice Website) (0:23–0:25)
College Guides (.edu: U.S.News Colleges and Careers Center) (0:25–0:32)
Rankings (0:32–0:37)
Other Resources to Help You Plan, Decide, and Apply (0:37–0:40)

TESTS

College Board Online (0:40–0:46)
Other Testing Resources (0:46–0:48)

FINANCES AND FINANCIAL AID

Overview (0:48–0:52)
The Student Guide: Financial Aid from the U.S. Department of Education (0:52–0:58)
Other Financial Aid Resources (0:58–1:00)

ADULT EDUCATION AND DISTANCE LEARNING

Introduction (1:00–1:02)
Arragon.com: Linking Adults to Learning (1:02–1:08)
Other Adult Education and Distance Learning Resources (1:08–1:09)

OTHER SOURCES OF INFORMATION (1:09–1:12)

REVIEW (1:12–1:15)

SAMPLE SCRIPT

Because this is largely a lecture/demonstration class, the challenge is to get and keep the attendees interested and involved. It is important, therefore, to ask questions and get attendees to participate as much as you can. In addition, try to walk around the room, among the audience; don't hide behind a lectern.

Also, be aware that Web site design invariably changes over time. Be sure to review any parts of this script that refer to specific aspects of a site's layout or navigation, and make any necessary updates.

Introduction

WELCOME (0:00–0:01)

Good evening! Who wants to go to college?

[Raise your hand to indicate that they should raise their hands if they wish.]

Well, I hope nearly everyone here is at least thinking about it, or is a parent of someone who is, because tonight we are going to talk about how to use the Internet in your college search. Let's begin!

PREREQUISITES (0:01–0:02)

First, I want to make sure everybody is in the right place. This demonstration assumes that you have already taken our "Getting Started on the World Wide Web" workshop, or that you already have a basic understanding of the Web and how to search it. We're just going to take that as a given. Does anyone have any questions about that?

OBJECTIVES (0:02–0:05)

OK, we have three objectives for this demonstration.

[Have the three objectives already written on a flip chart or board.]

At the end of this hour, you will be able to (1) explain the various types of college information resources on the Web; (2) use specific resources of each type effectively and incorporate them into your college planning and application process; and (3) apply your knowledge to the learning and use of new college information resources, particularly those on the handouts [pages 132–137] for this session.

Please keep in mind that our focus here will be on the Internet. But there are many other college information resources available to you, and we'll talk a little bit about those later.

Let's start!

Colleges and Universities

INTRODUCTION (0:05–0:08)

One of the best ways to get information about colleges and universities is to go right to the source—to these institutions' Web sites. Let's start with that.

Just about every college or university maintains a Web site these days. All of them look a little different and are organized in a unique way, but most of them have pretty similar information: an overview and history of the school; profiles of students and faculty; academic programs and departments; listings of classes; information about the library and computing resources; student groups and sports; and information on the application process.

In many ways, these Web sites are like extensive online brochures for colleges and universities. As with a brochure, they can contain great information. It's also important to remember that, like a brochure, they strive to portray the college in the best light possible: they'll use the prettiest pictures of the campus, the most positive quotes from students. They are advertisements.

But also, in some ways, they are better than print brochures. For one thing, they are often more extensive than a print brochure, since they are not as limited in terms of space. This means, for instance, that if you are really interested in, say, engineering or art as your major, you will likely find that these individual departments have their own sections on the Web site with a lot of great information. Moreover, you can start to get a flavor of what a school is like even without visiting. For example, student groups on campus very often have their own home pages on the college or university sites, as will individual students. So, for instance, if you are interested in political groups or literary magazines on campus, you can probably find their home pages linked from the main college or university site.

YAHOO SEARCH (0:08–0:13)

So let's visit one. How do you find a particular college or university Web site? Well, one way is to guess the address; often, you will guess right. Who can guess the address for [*name a college or university in your area or state, with an obvious URL, such as* http://www.purdue.edu *or* http://www.colorado.edu]?

[*Get responses.*]

So guessing the address and just typing it in and trying it will often work, if you remember, of course, to end the address with the .edu extension given to colleges and other educational organizations. But it doesn't always; sometimes Web addresses are not so obvious. What I suggest, then, is that you turn to a directory that lists and provides links for most if not all of the college and university Web sites. One of the best, and one which many of you probably know about already, is the first one on your handout: Yahoo (*http:// www.yahoo.com/Regional/Countries/United_States/Education/Colleges_and_ Universities/*). I am going to go there now.

[*Click on the link or type the address, and click down to Yahoo's listing of colleges and universities.*]

By the way, all the sites I am going to demonstrate today are listed on your handouts, so don't worry about having to copy down any addresses.

Here is Yahoo's very comprehensive listing of colleges and universities in the United States. As you see, they have some special sections, for instance on community colleges, women's colleges, and historically black colleges. You can also get a complete listing of all the colleges and universities, which I would not recommend doing since it is so long. Instead, you can just click on the first letter of the name of the school you are interested in. I am going to click on the letter A.

[*Select the letter A.*]

This brings me to a list of all the colleges and universities that begin with the letter A. Easy!

SAMPLE COLLEGE WEB SITE (0:13–0:20)

Let's take a quick look at one college site to get an idea of the kinds of information that are usually available. I am already on the A list, so I am going to pick Auburn University.

[*Select the Auburn link.*]

[*Auburn University is simply an example. It would be a good idea to choose a college or university in your area or state to demonstrate. Alternately, you could ask for an audience suggestion for a school to look at. Although it is impossible to plan the search and this may slow down the session, the risk is not too great because most college and university sites have similar content.*]

As you see, Yahoo provides links to some related sites and subsections of the Auburn University site: alumni organizations, libraries and museums, and so on. The main link to the Auburn home page is the one at the top. I'll choose that one.

[Select the Auburn link.]

Here you see the home page for Auburn University. It is a pretty typical college or university home page. As you see, it sort of looks like an online brochure. There are pretty pictures of students studying under trees, and it is all very attractively designed.

It is also full of information, and the information you find here is typical of a college or university Web site. There are a variety of buttons at the top that will lead you to further information. For instance, under Academics, you will find information about the various departments and programs of study at Auburn, including a complete course listing and faculty information. Under Student Life, you will find information on student activities and housing, and the section on Organizations has information about every organization on campus. The section on Athletics has information on the various sports teams and programs. All of this is similar to what you'll find on most college and university Web sites.

Every college and university Web site will probably also have a section on Admissions; after all, they want you to apply. Auburn is no different; let's briefly take a look at that.

[Select the Admissions link.]

Here you see that they offer information about undergraduate admissions, graduate admissions, financial aid, registration, and scholarships. I am going to select Undergraduate Admissions.

[Select the Undergraduate Admissions link.]

Here you will find information about requirements, answers to frequently asked questions about the application process, and information on application deadlines. Also, notice here that you can download a copy of the application form itself.

It used to be that the only way you could apply to college was to call or write the admissions office and ask them to send you an application; you would then fill it out and mail it back to them. Well, you can still do that, and many times there will be a place on the college's Web site to request that they mail you an application.

In addition, these days you can often download an application directly from a college's Web site or from a service that they use. Sometimes they'll ask you to mail in the completed application, and sometimes you can e-mail it to them or even fill the application out directly online. And these days many colleges and universities accept what is known as a "Common Application," which is a standard application that can be used at a number of different schools.

Each college has its own methods and rules, so the best thing is check its Web site under Admissions or Applications.

Similarly, under the Financial Aid section of a college's Web site, in addition to finding out about the various financial aid opportunities at that particular school, you can often download a financial aid application, or request to have one sent to you. We are going to talk more about financial aid resources in a few minutes.

OTHER COLLEGE AND UNIVERSITY SITES (0:20–0:23)

We have seen the kinds of information and resources that are offered on college and university Web sites. And probably the best way to find these Web sites is to do a quick search on Yahoo, which is listed at the top of your handout. Also on your handout, going down the list, there are some other directories of college and university Web sites: American Universities (*http://www.clas.ufl.edu/CLAS/american-universities.html*); College and University Home Pages (*http://www.mit.edu:8001/people/cdemello/univ.html*); University Links (*http://www-net.com/univ/univ-t.html*); and The Center for All Collegiate Information (*http://www.collegiate.net/*).

In addition, the American Association of Community Colleges (*http://www.aacc.nche.edu/*), Community College Web (*http://www.mcli.dist.maricopa.edu/cc/*), and U.S. Two-Year Colleges (*http://www.sp.utoledo.edu/twoyrcol.html*) provide directories of community and two-year colleges throughout the United States. Vocational Education Resources (*http://pegasus.cc.ucf.edu/~sorg/vocation.html*) provides an annotated directory of resources related to vocational education.

The Association of Universities and Colleges of Canada (*http://www.aucc.ca/*) and Canadian Universities (*http://www.uwaterloo.ca/canu/index.html*) offer directories of Canadian colleges and universities. Studyabroad.com (*http://www.studyabroad.com/*) offers an extensive directory of study-abroad programs in more than 100 countries.

And finally, on a somewhat lighter note, the College Nicknames site (*http://www.afn.org/~recycler/sports.html*) provides an alphabetical list of college nicknames, and the GreekPages (*http://www.greekpages.com/*) offers a directory of fraternities and sororities on the Web.

I encourage you to explore some of these resources on your own after this demonstration or at a later date.

Planning, Deciding, and Applying

OVERVIEW (COLLEGE CHOICE WEBSITE) (0:23–0:25)

So we have seen the kinds of information that colleges and universities offer on their Web sites. And this information can certainly help when you are trying to decide among different schools. But let's step back: How do you decide what kind of college to go to in the first place? Do you want a community college? A public university? A private college or university? What size college do you want to attend? And there are many other factors to consider, including academic reputation, location, selectivity, cost and financial aid options, academic programs, student demographics, and social life and activities.

Usually you will want to start seriously investigating colleges during your junior year, so that you can be filling out applications during the fall of your senior year. But how can you get help sorting through the process?

Well, there are a number of college guides on the Web that can help you. One site that I would like to mention but that we won't look at today is the College Choice Website (*http://www.gseis.ucla.edu/mm/cc/home.html*). It is on your handout. This site is a great introduction to the whole process. It walks you through all the steps, including preparing for college, selecting a school, the application process, and financing. It even has a timeline, telling you what to do when. I really encourage you to take a look at this site and use it as a guide.

COLLEGE GUIDES (.EDU: U.S. NEWS COLLEGES AND CAREERS CENTER) (0:25–0:32)

There are also many professionally produced college guides on the Web that contain information about preparing, applying, and financing, and that also have profiles of specific schools. Let's look at one of these now. It's from *U.S. News & World Report* and is called .edu: U.S.News Colleges and Careers Center (*http://www4.usnews.com/usnews/edu/*).

[Select the link or type the address.]

One of the best-known features of *U.S. News* is its rankings of colleges and universities, and these rankings are available from the site. We will return to rankings in a few minutes.

U.S. News also offers a wealth of introductory and background material on the college selection and application process. Under the Get Into College and Financial Aid buttons in the upper right corner, you will find some very useful essays and guides to help you through the entire process. There is also information for parents.

But the heart of the site is its directory of profiles of over 1,400 colleges and universities throughout the country. Let's take a look at one to see the kinds of information offered. I will click on Find a College.

[Select the Find a College link.]

Here I have a couple of options. I can simply search by a school's name. I can also search for schools that match certain criteria, including location, cost, size, selectivity, majors offered, student/faculty ratio, academic programs, single-sex or coed, religious affiliation, campus setting, ranking, extracurricular activities, and sports. This is a great way to become aware of schools that match some of your interests and selection criteria.

In the interest of time, let's simply search for a school by name. Let's look at a school that someone here is interested in. Who would like to volunteer a school, and we'll take a look at that?

[Have a volunteer name a school and use that as your sample search. If no one volunteers, call on someone. We will use Dartmouth College as our example.]

So what we do is type all or part of the school's name into the search box. I will type in *Dartmouth*.

[Search for Dartmouth.]

And I get two results: University of Massachusetts—Dartmouth and Dartmouth College. Dartmouth College is the one I want, so I will select that.

[Select the Dartmouth College link.]

This brings us to the profile for Dartmouth College. This profile is similar to ones you get from college guidebooks in print.

The first section is called At a Glance and offers basic information, such as address, Web site address, religious affiliation, size, campus setting, application deadline, *U.S. News* ranking, and basic expense information.

Some of the other sections of the college profile, available under the links in the upper left corner, delve into these areas a little more deeply. For instance, if I select Admissions . . .

[Select the Admissions link.]

. . . this offers me further information about deadlines, application fees, types of applications accepted, acceptance rates, tests required, average test scores, and other information.

If I select Academics . . .

[Select the Academics link.]

. . . this offers me information on majors offered, study abroad programs, class size, student-to-faculty ratio, graduation rate, and other resources.

And, you see, there are similar areas for Financial Aid, Ranking, Student Body, Services, Campus Life, Extracurriculars, International Students, Transfer Applicants, and Disabled Students.

RANKINGS (0:32–0:37)

Now, let's talk about rankings a little bit. *U.S. News & World Report* is known for its college and university rankings. Every year the magazine produces lists of rankings of various types of schools: national universities, national liberal arts colleges, regional colleges, and universities. These rankings are also available on its Web site.

[Select the College Rankings link.]

U.S. News ranks schools for academic quality and uses a number of different criteria, including academic reputation, student selectivity, faculty resources, retention rate, financial resources, alumni giving, and graduation rate. It gives various weights to these different criteria, gathers data using a number of surveys, and then ranks the schools according to the results.

Now, the *U.S. News* rankings get a lot of publicity, but they also generate a lot of controversy. Many people question the validity of the *U.S. News* data, and many people also do not agree with the whole enterprise of trying to compare and rank schools.

For a discussion of the controversy of college rankings, along with links to a number of other rankings lists and to the *U.S. News* list, try the site from the University of Illinois called College and University Rankings (*http:// www.library.uiuc.edu/edx/rankings.htm*).

[Select the link or type the address.]

In addition to its annotated list of rankings, this site offers links to articles about how to use rankings in your college selection process. No matter how you feel about rankings, this much is clear: it should only be one element in your selection process, and you should use rankings with a grain of salt. You have to find the college that has the right mix of qualities and programs for you, and no ranking service can tell you that.

OTHER RESOURCES TO HELP YOU PLAN, DECIDE, AND APPLY (0:37–0:40)

There are a lot of other Web sites that can help you in the process of planning for college, choosing the colleges you are interested in, and applying. Many of these are listed on your handout.

For an excellent general college guide on the Web, try Petersons.com (*http:// www.petersons.com/*). You might be familiar with the Peterson's college guide book. Its online counterpart also provides overview information on schools and colleges, along with an application service and other resources. Other college guides on the Web include CollegeEdge (*http://www.collegeedge.com/*), Money Online: College Guide (*http://www.pathfinder.com/@fwqMBwcAef6ViVHy/ money/colleges98/*), and CollegeNet (*http://www.collegenet.com/*).

Adventures in Education (*http://adventuresineducation.org/*) offers guidance on selecting a school, the application process, financing, and career choice, and Mapping Your Future (*http://mapping-your-future.org/*) offers information on choosing a college, paying for it, and planning a career.

The Maclean's Universities site (*http://www.macleans.ca/pipeline/unimag/ excel.html*) provides rankings for Canadian colleges and universities, and Critical Comparisons of American Colleges and Universities (*http://www.memex- press.com/cc/*) offers comparative data on U.S. colleges and universities.

And finally, CampusTours: Virtual College Tours (*http://www.campustours. com/*) offers links to college Web sites that include virtual tours, campus maps, and "Webcam" video cameras. It's a great way to visit a college without having to buy a plane ticket!

Tests

COLLEGE BOARD ONLINE (0:40–0:46)

OK, we all know that one element of applying to college—perhaps not the most pleasant one—is taking the SAT test, and maybe some other tests, as well. How many of you have taken the PSAT or the SAT already?

Well, the College Board (*http://www.collegeboard.org/*), which is the organization that administers the tests, has a very useful Web site. Let's take a look at that now.

[Select the link or type the address.]

You'll see near the top that they have information for Students & Parents. I'll select that.

[Select the link for Students & Parents.]

Here we find some information similar to what we have seen before—for example, a guide on planning for college. But the most important feature of the College Board site is its test information. Here, under Getting Ready for the Tests, you can find SAT test-taking tips and sample questions that can help you prepare.

You also see information on each of the individual tests: the PSAT, the SAT, the AP (Advanced Placement) tests, and the CLEP Exams for college credit. Under the SAT, for instance, you can register for the test online. Let's look at that.

[Select the link for Register Online.]

This first page offers basic information about how to register online. You will need a credit card. If you want to pay by check or money order, you will have to register by mail. We are using a "Secure Browser," which means that it is safe to send your credit card information online. I'll choose the Register for the SAT Using a Secure Browser link.

[Select the link for Register for the SAT Using a Secure Browser.]

That brings us to the SAT registration page. This page is an easy-to-complete online registration form. I won't walk us through it, because it takes a little time, but it is very self-explanatory. You fill in your name, address, telephone number, birthday, gender, social security number, current grade level, expected graduation date, and your high school code (it allows you to search for your high school code online if you don't know it).

You then select the test you want to take (SAT I or SAT II), your test date, and your test center (again, it allows you to search for test center codes online). You can also search for and select the codes designating colleges and scholarship programs to which you wish to send your scores.

It then gives you information about the fees and prompts you for your credit card information. As I said, this is a secure process, so you shouldn't worry about entering this information. If this bothers you, though, you can always register using the paper form.

OTHER TESTING RESOURCES (0:46–0:48)

There are other sources on the Web for test help and information, and these are on your handout. You may have heard of Kaplan (*http://www.kaplan.com/*) and the Princeton Review (*http://www.review.com/*). These are the two big commercial test preparation companies; for a fee, they offer test preparation classes and other materials. A lot of the information on their Web sites is about the classes they offer, but you can also find some free help, including practice questions and sample tests.

And finally, the GRE OnLine (*http://www.gre.org/*) is similar to the College Board and offers similar information, except it is for graduate school.

Finances and Financial Aid

OVERVIEW (0:48–0:52)

One of the biggest concerns about going to college is how to pay for it. College can be very expensive. Costs include tuition, room and board, books, transportation, and other miscellaneous fees and expenses.

However, there are many financial aid options available to you. About half of all college students receive some form of financial aid. So don't let the high costs of going to college stop you!

There are three basic kinds of financial aid:

[Have these already written on a flip chart or board.]

- *Scholarships or grants.* These awards do not have to be paid back and can be based on merit, need, or both.
- *Loans.* Loans have to be paid back and are based on need. However, student loans often have good interest rates and do not have to be paid back until after school is completed.
- *Work study.* This is where the student works to help defray college costs.

There are also a variety of sources of financial aid. For example, the federal government offers grants, loans, and work study programs. ROTC is another example of a government program. Colleges and universities offer a number of grants and scholarships, both need- and merit-based, directly to students. And other sources of financial help can include local organizations, businesses, and individuals.

How do you learn about all the financial aid opportunities?

THE STUDENT GUIDE: FINANCIAL AID FROM THE U.S. DEPARTMENT OF EDUCATION (0:52–0:58)

Well, for one thing, keep your ears open, talk to your guidance counselor at school, and read the information about financial aid provided by the colleges and universities you are interested in. And on the Web, an excellent place to start is The Student Guide: Financial Aid from the U.S. Department of Education (*http://www.ed.gov/prog_info/SFA/StudentGuide/*). Let's look at that now.

[Select the link or type the address.]

Approximately two-thirds of all financial aid to students comes from programs administered by the U.S. Department of Education, and The Student Guide is the most comprehensive resource for information on all of these programs. It is available in print as well as on the Web; we have copies available here at the library.

[Show copies, or tell where they can be located.]

You can also call the toll-free number provided on the Web site to have a free copy sent to you at home. Let's look at their Web site.

[Click through to the Introduction/Contents page.]

I am on the introductory page, which offers a table of contents for what is available in this guide. You see that there are general information sections, and then sections on specific programs, such as Pell Grants, Stafford Loans, and PLUS Loans. Each of these sections gives you an introduction to the financial aid program, along with information on eligibility, payment, and the application process.

Notice that there is a section on Applying. I'll click on that now.

[Select the link for Applying.]

This section offers a great introduction to the application process, including an overview of the Free Application for Federal Student Aid (FAFSA). This is the standard form you need to fill out to apply for federal financial aid. You can even apply directly on the Internet, and they offer a link here. You can also download a free software program that allows you to apply; you can have your school submit your application, or you can request a paper application and mail it in.

I really encourage you to start your research into financial aid with the Student Guide from the U.S. Department of Education. It is written in plain language, is easy to understand, and offers great information.

OTHER FINANCIAL AID RESOURCES (0:58–1:00)

I want to mention a few other financial aid information resources that are listed on your handout.

In particular, I'd like to call your attention to FinAid: The Financial Aid Information Page (*http://www.finaid.org/*). This is probably the next site to turn to after looking at the Department of Education's Student Guide. FinAid offers a useful overview of financial aid and a glossary of financial aid terms. It also includes an extensive, annotated directory of links to financial aid sources and information on the Web. It is particularly good on nongovernment sources of aid, and special interest resources, such as loan and scholarship programs available to minority students, female students, athletes, and other groups.

Other financial aid resources include the Nellie Mae Web site (*http:// www.nelliemae.com/*), which offers information on student loans, and fastWEB! (*http://www.fastweb.com/*), which provides a searchable database of more than 180,000 U.S. scholarships, internships, grants, and loans. The Education Funding Web site from Prudential (*http://www.prudential.com/edufunding/*) includes excellent information on college costs, including a calculator to help determine necessary savings. And don't forget the sites we covered in the "Planning, Deciding, and Applying" section; many of them also include financing and financial aid information.

Adult Education and Distance Learning

INTRODUCTION (1:00–1:02)

Last, I want us to turn to adult education and distance learning. Today, more and more adults are returning to school, either to work toward a degree or certificate, or simply to attend classes to learn a new skill, broaden their knowledge, or pursue an interest. In addition, many people are taking classes and getting an education entirely online; they don't attend school in person at all. This is often called distance education or distance learning.

ARRAGON.COM: LINKING ADULTS TO LEARNING (1:02–1:08)

One of the best places to learn about these educational opportunities is a site called Arragon.com: Linking Adults to Learning (*http://www.arragon.com/*). Let's look at that one now.

[Select the link or type the address.]

The educational programs on this site are geared toward working adults— usually the programs are offered part-time, during evenings, and/or on weekends. And Arragon.com includes information for many different types of programs: degree programs (associate, undergraduate, and graduate); certificates; single classes; executive programs; and distance education (which may comprise any of the above).

Let's do a sample search. The easiest way to search Arragon.com is to select Click Here at the top to do a search for programs in your area. I'll do that now.

[Select the Click Here link.]

Here we can choose to search for programs near a zip code. Let's pick our own zip code; I'll type that in now.

[Type in a local zip code and tailor the following search accordingly. Be sure to plan this in advance. We will use 98102 as an example.]

After I type in the zip code *98102*, I select the type of program I want. Let's say I am interested only in bachelor and associate degree programs. I can check both of those boxes.

[Select the Bachelor Degrees and Associate Degrees boxes.]

Next I need to type in key words for what I am interested in studying. Let's say I am interested in graphic design. I will type those words in the box.

[Type graphic design into the search box. Alternately, you can ask your audience if there is a type of program they are interested in learning about.]

I click the Find button to perform my search . . .

[Click Find button.]

. . . and this brings me back to my results. The results list gives me the titles of the programs, the colleges, and the beginnings of the descriptions. I can click on individual programs to get more information. For instance, if I click on the first one (Graphic Design and Illustration at Seattle Central Community College) . . .

[Select the link.]

. . . I get a profile of the degree program, a list of classes, a telephone contact number, and a link to the school's Web site. After you find out about programs using the Arragon.com Web site, you should always check with the school directly to find out more, request a catalog, and learn about application procedures.

OTHER ADULT EDUCATION AND DISTANCE LEARNING RESOURCES (1:08–1:09)

There are a number of other resources on the Web to learn about adult education and distance learning opportunities, and these are included on your handout. If you are interested, I encourage you to check out some of these in addition to Arragon.com.

Other Sources of Information (1:09–1:12)

We have covered a lot of ground on the Web today, and we're about done, but I want to mention that there are, of course, a lot of sources of college information that are *not* on the Web.

Undoubtedly the most useful resource is *people*. In particular, your guidance counselor at school and your parents or guardians are the best people to turn to for information and advice. Your guidance counselor might also have books and college choice software programs that can help you. Also, teachers, your parents' friends, older brothers and sisters, your own friends: all of these folks can have information and opinions to offer. Some people also hire independent guidance counselors.

And don't forget about books! The library has an excellent collection of printed college guides.

[Show a couple of examples and/or point out where the collection is located.]

You can also call or write the colleges and universities themselves and have them send you a catalog and a brochure, or you can often request these online. And you may want to visit a few colleges, either before you decide where to apply or after you have been accepted and are trying to decide which one to attend. You can usually have an interview when you visit, which may either be an informational interview or one element of the application process. Finally, there are often college fairs that you can attend locally and meet representatives from a number of different colleges at the same time.

Review (1:12–1:15)

Let's just quickly review what we have gone over today.

First we talked about college and university Web sites themselves, and all of the information they offer: information about academics, admissions, applications, financial aid, college life on campus. And what is a good way to find a college or university site?

[Get responses.]

Yes, Yahoo is an easy way to find college and university home pages, and guessing the address often works, too.

Next we looked at some resources to help you plan and decide. The *U.S. News* site has in-depth profiles of colleges and universities. It also has a famous rankings listing, which can be useful but should be considered with a grain of salt.

Then we talked about the SAT test, and looked at the College Board site, which has some sample questions and also allows you to register online.

Next we turned to finances and financial aid. We learned that most students received financial aid to help them attend college, and most student financial aid comes from the federal government. We looked at The Student Guide, from the U.S. Department of Education, which gives an overview of all the government's financial aid programs, and allows you to fill out the Free Application for Federal Financial Aid right online.

And finally, we talked about adult education and distance learning. Many people are working toward degrees or taking classes in these types of programs, and Arragon.com is a great site to use to learn about these opportunities.

The college planning, decision, and application process is a long one, and it requires a lot of time and research. I hope you've seen that the Web can really be a big help in that process, along with guidance counselors, friends, and printed college guides. Thanks so much for coming today. Does anyone have any questions?

COLLEGE INFORMATION ON THE WEB AGENDA

Introduction

- Welcome
- Prerequisites
- Objectives

Colleges and Universities

- Introduction
- Yahoo Search
- Sample College Web Site
- Other College and University Sites

Planning, Deciding, and Applying

- Overview (College Choice Website)
- College Guides (.edu: U.S. News Colleges and Careers Center)
- Rankings
- Other Resources to Help You Plan, Decide, and Apply

Tests

- College Board Online
- Other Testing Resources

Finances and Financial Aid

- Overview
- The Student Guide: Financial Aid from the U.S. Department of Education
- Other Financial Aid Resources

Adult Education and Distance Learning

- Introduction
- Arragon.com: Linking Adults to Learning
- Other Adult Education and Distance Learning Resources

Other Sources of Information

Review

COLLEGE INFORMATION ON THE WEB: USEFUL SITES

The following are Web sites covered in this training session . . . and a few other useful sites. They follow the order of the workshop.

Colleges and Universities

Yahoo: Colleges and Universities in the United States
http://www.yahoo.com/Regional/Countries/United_States/Education/Colleges_and_Universities/
Yahoo's complete listing of college and university Web sites.

American Universities
http://www.clas.ufl.edu/CLAS/american-universities.html
An alphabetically arranged list of links to colleges and universities in the United States.

College and University Home Pages
http://www.mit.edu:8001/people/cdemello/univ.html
Provides links to college and university Web sites throughout the world.

University Links
http://www-net.com/univ/univ-t.html
Provides links to colleges and universities in the United States, sorted by type, alphabet, and location.

The Center for All Collegiate Information
http://www.collegiate.net/
Provides links to many types of college Web sites, including departmental and sports pages.

American Association of Community Colleges
http://www.aacc.nche.edu/
Includes links to member colleges listed by state.

Community College Web
http://www.mcli.dist.maricopa.edu/cc/
Provides a searchable index of community college Web sites, along with other resources.

U.S. Two-Year Colleges
http://www.sp.utoledo.edu/twoyrcol.html
An extensive list of two-year colleges in the United States, searchable by state.

Vocational Education Resources
http://pegasus.cc.ucf.edu/~sorg/vocation.html
An annotated directory of resources related to vocational education.

Association of Universities and Colleges of Canada
http://www.aucc.ca/
Includes a directory of Canadian colleges and universities.

Canadian Universities
http://www.uwaterloo.ca/canu/index.html
Information about studying in Canada, and links to Canadian universities.

COLLEGE INFORMATION ON THE WEB: USEFUL SITES—(CONTINUED)

studyabroad.com

http://www.studyabroad.com/

Extensive, searchable directory of study-abroad programs in more than 100 countries.

College Nicknames

http://www.afn.org/~recycler/sports.html

An alphabetical list of college nicknames.

GreekPages

http://www.greekpages.com/

An extensive directory of fraternities and sororities on the Web. Can be searched by college and chapter.

Planning, Deciding, and Applying

College Choice Website

http://www.gseis.ucla.edu/mm/cc/home.html

An excellent introduction to preparing for college and selecting a school, and to the application process.

.edu: U.S. News Colleges and Careers Center

http://www4.usnews.com/usnews/edu/

Includes profiles of schools, rankings, application information, financial aid resources, and more.

College and University Rankings

http://www.library.uiuc.edu/edx/rankings.htm

An extensive annotated directory of college ranking sites. Also includes a list of print resources.

Petersons.com

http://www.petersons.com/

Information on schools and colleges; an application service; and other resources.

CollegeEdge

http://www.collegeedge.com/

Includes profiles of schools, an application service, advice on choosing a college, and other resources.

Money Online: College Guide

http://www.pathfinder.com/@fwqMBwcAef6ViVHy/money/colleges98/

Includes profiles of four-year colleges, plus a savings calculator.

CollegeNet

http://www.collegenet.com/

Allows users to search for schools by various criteria. Also includes an application service.

Adventures in Education

http://adventuresineducation.org/

Offers guidance on selecting a school, the application process, financing, and career choice.

Mapping Your Future

http://mapping-your-future.org/

Provides information on choosing a college, paying for it, and planning a career.

Maclean's Universities

http://www.macleans.ca/pipeline/unimag/excel.html

Provides rankings of Canadian colleges and universities.

Critical Comparisons of American Colleges and Universities

http://www.memex-press.com/cc/

Comparative data on colleges and universities from the U.S. Department of Education and other sources.

CampusTours: Virtual College Tours

http://www.campustours.com/

Provides links to college Web sites that include virtual tours, campus maps, and Webcams.

Tests

College Board Online

http://www.collegeboard.org/

Offers online registration, a schedule of test dates, test preparation, and more.

Kaplan

http://www.kaplan.com/

Information from this commercial test preparation service, including practice questions.

Princeton Review Online

http://www.review.com/

Another commercial test preparation service providing information and sample tests.

GRE OnLine

http://www.gre.org/

Includes information on the GRE tests for graduate school, including dates, registration, and sample test questions.

Finances and Financial Aid

The Student Guide: Financial Aid from the U.S. Department of Education

http://www.ed.gov/prog_info/SFA/StudentGuide/

Includes information on grants, loans, and work-study available through the federal Student Financial Assistance Programs.

FinAid: The Financial Aid Information Page

http://www.finaid.org/

Provides an overview of financial aid and an extensive, annotated directory of links to financial aid sources and information on the Web.

Nellie Mae

http://www.nelliemae.com/

Provides information on student loans.

COLLEGE INFORMATION ON THE WEB: USEFUL SITES—(CONTINUED)

fastWEB! (Financial Aid Search through the Web)

http://www.fastweb.com/

Provides a searchable database of more than 180,000 U.S. scholarships, internships, grants, and loans.

Education Funding

http://www.prudential.com/edufunding/

Provides information on college costs. Includes a calculator to help determine necessary savings.

See also the sites listed above under "Planning, Deciding, and Applying"; many of them also include financing and financial aid information.

Adult Education and Distance Learning

Arragon.com: Linking Adults to Learning

http://www.arragon.com/

Provides links to education programs for working adults (including degree, certificate, executive and distance learning programs), along with individual classes.

Peterson's: Distance Learning

http://www.petersons.com/dlearn/

Peterson's directory of distance learning programs.

CollegeDegree.com

http://www.collegedegree.com/

Offers a searchable directory of distance education programs.

I Got My Degree through E-Mail

http://www.forbes.com/forbes/97/0616/5912084a.htm

A *Forbes* magazine article about distance education programs. Includes links to resources and programs.

The Distance and Education Training Council Online

http://www.detc.org/

Provides a directory of accredited distance education institutions.

The World Lecture Hall

http://www.utexas.edu/world/lecture/

Provides links to Web pages created by faculty worldwide. Includes syllabi, reading lists, lecture notes, and other class materials.

Spectrum Virtual University

http://www.vu.org/

Offers a variety of free classes online.

FURTHER READING

Cochrane, Kerry. *Researching Colleges on the World Wide Web*. New York: Franklin Watts, 1997.
   Provides an overview of how to use the Web in every step of the college selection and application process.
Karl, Shannon, and Arthur Karl. *How to Get into Your Dream College Using the Web*. Albany, N.Y.: Coriolis Group Books, 1997.
   Provides advice on the selection and application process. Includes companion CD with links to other resources.

8
Introduction to HTML (Part 1): Structure and Text

Handouts for this worskop follow page 197.

OVERVIEW

Who

This series of HTML training workshops is designed for library staff members who have no experience with HTML; the series is general enough, though, to be offered to anyone, including patrons. They must, however, be comfortable using the Web, a word processor, and Windows (or whatever operating system you will be using). The staff members must take these workshops in order. These employees may be asked to contribute to the development of the library's Web site in the future, or they may simply want to know more about Web development technology.

What

This series of three hands-on workshops provides a basic introduction to

HTML. Part 1 provides an overview of HTML and introduces basic structural and textual presentation tags.

Clearly, it is impossible to provide thorough training on all aspects of HTML and Web development technology and design in three one-hour workshops, so these workshops should be seen as the first three of what could be an extensive (perhaps ongoing) training series on Web development technology. Potentially fruitful future one-hour workshops in the series could focus on:

- Tables
- Frames
- META tags and designing for search engines
- Design issues
- Uploading and local editorial procedures
- Imagemaps
- Multimedia (audio and video)
- Cascading Style Sheets
- Dynamic HTML (DHTML)
- Common Gateway Interface (CGI) and database technology
- Portable Document Format (PDF)
- Extensible Markup Language (XML)

Some of these workshops would be highly technical and advanced; for a general audience, they might work better as informational lectures rather than hands-on workshops.

Even for this initial three-part series, you will need approval from the trainees' managers, not only for participation during the sessions but also so that the staff members are given time to complete their out-of-class assignments. You will need to obtain this approval prior to conducting the training series.

In addition to the handouts, you will need a floppy disk for each person. You could also instruct participants to bring one of their own, but you will need to have spares in case anyone forgets.

Where

This training session is designed for a computer lab with space for ten students and an instructor (11 PCs total). The instructor's PC has projection. Each of the computers has Internet access, Microsoft Internet Explorer (or another graphical browser), Windows 95 or Windows 98 (this workshop can be adapted easily to another operating system), and Notepad (or another plain text editor).

When

Attendees should be required to complete all three sessions in this series in sequence. This session lasts one hour.

Why

The objectives of this three-part series are for the trainees to be able to (1) explain the concepts of HTML; (2) create basic Web pages using correct HTML (text, links, and graphics); and (3) use appropriate resources effectively for further learning and reference.

The objectives for Part 1 are for the trainees to be able to (1) explain the concepts of HTML; (2) use basic structural and textual presentation HTML tags; and (3) begin to turn to appropriate resources to learn more about textual presentation tags.

The major unstated objectives of this session (and of the HTML series as a whole) are to make the trainees excited about the technology and to motivate them to learn more. One way to do this is to demonstrate how easy it is to create basic Web pages; that is why the workshops are hands-on and designed so that the trainees have a finished product of their own creation at the end. Some of your trainees will want to stop at the end of the three-part series; they will have learned as much as interests them. Others will be motivated to keep going and learn as much as they can. This series accommodates both kinds of learners.

WORKSHOP AGENDA

This agenda moves quickly into hands-on creation of HTML documents. Because all the material will be new to the trainees, and because they will be typing the tags, this can be a slow process. Nevertheless, it is worth it; the most effective and rewarding way for them to learn is to create actual HTML pages. Since this is a hands-on class, it would help (although it's not necessary) to have an assistant, who can aid anyone who gets stuck and falls behind.

Outline

INTRODUCTION (0:00–0:05)

- Welcome
- Prerequisites
- Objectives for this Session

What Is HTML? (0:05–0:15)

- Definition
- View Source
- Tags

TOOLS (0:15–0:20)

- Text Editors
- HTML Editors/Web Authoring Tools
- Word Processors

BASIC STRUCTURAL TAGS (0:20–0:30)

- <HTML>
- <HEAD>
- <TITLE>
- <BODY>
- Save and View

OTHER STRUCTURAL AND PRESENTATION TAGS (0:30–0:40)

- Heading
- Paragraph
- Line Break
- Horizontal Rule

TEXT FORMATTING (0:40–0:50)

- Bold
- Italics
- Font: Size, Color, Face
- Logical Tags

ASSIGNMENT: LISTS (0:50–0:55)

- Lists: Unordered, Ordered, Definition
- Handouts (pages 198–200)

REVIEW AND WRAP UP (0:55–1:00)
- Copy Document to Hard Drive/Reminder to Bring Back Floppy
- Review

SAMPLE SCRIPT

This session is almost entirely hands-on. It is important, therefore, that everyone meet the prerequisites: competence in using the Web, a word processor, and Windows (or whatever operating system you are using).

This session assumes that you are using Internet Explorer, Windows 95 or Windows 98, and Notepad. If you have a different browser, operating system, or text editor, it will be easy to make the necessary alterations.

The hour will go quickly, and everyone will learn a lot in that time. However, you will not be able to cover everything about HTML, or even everything about the topics and tags in these lessons. You will cause confusion and get bogged down if you discuss every method of creating a particular effect in HTML. Concentrate on paring it down and sticking to essentials, even though you may have to leave out information about a particular tag or HTML feature.

Introduction (0:00–0:05)

WELCOME
Hello! Welcome to Part 1 in our three-part series "Introduction to HTML." After these three sessions, you will know the basics of how to create Web pages.

> [Optional: Introduce yourself and have others introduce themselves, if everyone doesn't know each other already.]

PREREQUISITES
The session will be hands-on, so I just want to make sure that everyone here already feels comfortable searching the Web, has experience using a word processor, and knows how to use Windows reasonably well. If you don't feel comfortable with all of that, or find yourself having some trouble when we get to the hands-on part, you might just want to look on with your neighbor. Does anyone have any questions about that?

OBJECTIVES

[Have the objectives for the three-part session written on a board or flip chart ahead of time.]

We have three objectives for this three-part introduction to HTML. After this series, you will be able to (1) explain the concepts of HTML; (2) create basic Web pages using correct HTML, including text, links, and graphics; and (3) use appropriate resources effectively for further learning and reference.

Today, we will focus on all three objectives. For the second objective, we will concentrate on structure and text. Part 2 will focus on links, and Part 3 will focus on graphics.

Let's begin!

What Is HTML? (0:05–0:15)

DEFINITION

Briefly, what is HTML? Well, as you probably know, it stands for Hypertext Markup Language, and, on a technical level, it is a convention based on the Standard Generalized Markup Language (SGML), a standard for publishing electronic documents. On a more practical level, HTML is simply a collection of "tags," and these tags tell the World Wide Web browser how to display a document.

VIEW SOURCE

Let's take a quick look at an HMTL document. Please open your Internet Explorer browsers *[modify for the browser you are using]* and go to the library's home page.

[For this demonstration, it is a nice idea to use your library's home page as an example, if it exists and seems appropriate. If not, choose another well-known or local site to demonstrate. Choose a site where the HTML code is fairly extensive, simple, and clear—not a page that is simply one image, or a page where the HTML is all jumbled together, for instance. We will use the Seattle Public Library as our example here.]

Here we have the Seattle Public Library's home page (*http://www.spl.lib.wa.us/*). Is everyone there?

Now, in your browser, at the top there is a menu option called View that I would like everyone to select. In the drop-down menu that appears, there is a choice to view the Source. Everyone please choose that.

You see that this opens up another window. What we are looking at is the HTML file for the Seattle Public Library's home page. This document tells the Web browser what to display: the text, the images, how the document looks, everything. This is what we are going to learn how to create in the next three sessions.

Tags

Notice in the source HTML document for Seattle Public Library all the things that are between angled brackets. For instance, near the top, there is <html> and <head> and <title>. And if you scroll down you'll see that this document is full of these things. Does everyone see that?

These elements in the angled brackets are the HTML tags that I mentioned a couple minutes ago. These tags are the heart of HTML and what we are going to learn how to create. Tags tell the Web browser what type of document this is, how to structure it, and how to display the text, links, images, and multimedia that are included. These tags have been established, defined, revised, and added to by standards groups and industry leaders, mainly the group known as the World Wide Web Consortium. Tags turn a plain text document into an HTML document for the Web.

You can go ahead and close the window showing the library home page's HTML source code. By the way, looking at the source code is a great way to learn about new HTML tags and Web design features; if you like the way something looks on any Web page, you can always look at the source code and find out how they did it!

Tools (0:15–0:20)

How do you create these HTML documents? A number of types of tools are available.

[*Have the three main types written on a board or flip chart ahead of time.*]

Text Editors

The most bare-bones option for HTML creation is to use the simple plain-text editor that comes with the operating system for your computer, such as Notepad for Windows and SimpleText for Macintosh. Using one of these text editors, you type all the tags yourself. HTML documents are created as plain-text, ASCII files, so this is a perfectly fine way to create HTML documents. Many people still write their HTML this way, and this is how we will do it throughout this series; it is the best way to learn the process and the tags.

HTML Editors/Web Authoring Tools

Typing out all the tags by hand, though, can be time-consuming, so tools have been created to speed up the process. For example, there are a number of HTML editors (both commercial and shareware) that have more of a button and menu approach to tagging. For instance, if you want to make something bold, you don't have to actually type the tag; you can, instead, highlight the text and then click the button for Bold. These HTML tagging editors can really speed up the process. Examples of this kind of HTML editor include HTML Assistant, Hot Dog, and Homesite.

Some other tools allow you to create documents in more of what is known as a WYSIWYG environment. WYSIWYG stands for "What You See Is What You Get." With these tools, you can do a lot of the Web page creation in a window that will actually look like the Web page. The program does the HTML coding for you. These kinds of tools are really good for folks who aren't interested in learning the underlying HTML coding. Examples of WYSIWYG tools are Microsoft's FrontPage and Adobe's PageMill. These commercial programs also have a lot of Web site management and graphics features.

Word Processors

Finally, standard word processors can be used to create HTML documents. One way to use a word processor is to use it simply like a text editor. You type out all the tags yourself, and then save your document as a text file (not a word file).

In addition, some word processors these days (Microsoft Word, for instance) allow you to save and convert documents to HTML files. It's a pretty nice feature, and allows you to work in a familiar word processing program and not deal with tagging.

As I said, though, we are going to do it the hard, old-fashioned way, for a few reasons. If you actually work with the coding, it's a better way to learn HTML itself; working with a text editor will give you a better understanding of what an HTML document is and how it functions. Also, it's still really useful to know HTML, since, even if you move on and start using a more sophisticated tool that does a lot of the tagging for you, you will often want to go in and tweak the HTML code. WYSIWIG programs won't do everything for you exactly the way you want it done. And finally, knowing HTML won't make you tool-dependent. Once you learn HTML, you can then easily learn any HTML editor or Web authoring tool. And you will always be able to use a simple text editor to create HTML documents, no matter where you are.

By the way, I will have a handout for you a little later, and that lists a number of resources for learning more about specific HTML and Web authoring tools.

Basic Structural Tags (0:20–0:30)

<HTML>

Let's create a Web page!

> *[You will do this along with everyone else, using projection so that everyone can see and follow along with you.]*

We should already have our browser open. Now we need to open Notepad in Windows.

> *[Modify for the operating system and text editor you are using, as appropriate.]*

This should be under the Start button in the lower left corner, then under Programs, and then Accessories. Then you should see Notepad and be able to choose and open that. Everyone got it open?

The first tags we are going to create define the basic document type and document structure.

First, document type. We need to tell the browser that this is an HTML document. We do that by using the HTML tag. Everyone do this on your machines in Notepad along with me. First we type the left angle bracket (<). All HTML tags begin with this left angle bracket. Then we type the tag name. In this case, it is HTML. Let's type that. And then we type a right angle bracket to close the tag. This leaves us with <HTML>. Everyone got that? All tags consist of this: a left angle bracket, a tag name, and a right angle bracket.

By the way, HTML tags are not case sensitive. You can type them either in upper or lower case, or a combination. I would suggest that you pick one or the other, though, and stick with it. It makes it look neater and is easier to read and spot mistakes. I write my tags in all uppercase; I think it's easier to spot them as I read through the HTML document. But it's up to you.

OK, we have created the first HTML tag, which tells the browser that what follows is going to be an HTML file. But we also need to put a closing tag at the end, to tell the browser that this is the end of the HTML document. Most HTML tags have both an opening tag and a closing tag; they usually come in pairs. Let's type the closing HTML tag now.

Do a couple of carriage returns after the opening HTML tag, just to give us some space. Then let's type the closing tag. Closing tags are the same as opening tags, except they have a backslash that goes before the tag name within the angle brackets. So the end HTML tag is </HTML>. Everyone got that?

Everything else we type will go between these two tags.

<HEAD>

OK, next we are going to define the basic structure of our document. HTML documents have two basic sections: the head and the body. The head contains the title. It can also contain some other elements that are for formatting and searching purposes only and don't actually appear in the browser; we won't go over those hidden elements now.

So let's type the HEAD tags. The start HEAD tag will go directly after the start HTML tag we created. Let's do another carriage return after that start HTML tag and type the HEAD tag on a new line. By the way, HTML does not recognize carriage returns or spaces. It doesn't matter at all whether you type new tags on the same line, a new line, or two lines down. The tags themselves are what define the spacing and how the document will look in the browser. But again, because I think it's easier to scan and troubleshoot the HTML document if new tags and new elements are on new lines, I usually do that. I suggest you do the same; it will just make it neater and easier to read in the long run.

I am going to type the start HEAD tag on the next line after the start HTML tag. This tag will look like this: <HEAD>. Everyone with me?

Next I am going to create the end HEAD tag on the next line. Similar to the end HTML tag we just typed, this will be </HEAD>. So now we all should have:

```
<HTML>
<HEAD>
</HEAD>
</HTML>
```

Everyone got that?

<TITLE>

Next, we need to put something in the head portion of our document. Often, the only thing that goes in the head portion is the title. The title is what appears in the title bar at the top of the browser window; it's usually that blue bar along the top. The title is also what search engines display in their results list, and, in fact, search engines use titles heavily when they are indexing documents. The title is also what is displayed in someone's Bookmarks or Favorites list. So it's important that we choose something that makes sense and that is relatively short.

First we need to create the start TITLE tag. This comes after the start HEAD tag. I am going to put it on a new line. The start TITLE tag is <TITLE>. Everyone with me?

Next, we type the actual text that will be our title. We will be creating our own individual home pages throughout this training, so I am going to call mine "Bill's Home Page."

[Modify this and future instructor elements to fit yourself.]

Go ahead and type that in, using your name instead of mine, of course.

And then we need to close this, using the closing TITLE tag. Can anyone guess what that is?

[Get responses.]

You got it. It's </TITLE>. Let's all type that in.

<BODY>

That's it for the head portion of our document. The other portion—the main portion of the document which will contain everything that will be displayed in the actual browser window—is the body portion of the document. Let's create the BODY tags now.

The opening BODY tag comes after the closing HEAD tag. Let's type that on a new line: <BODY>.

Then let's do a couple of carriage returns and type the closing BODY tag: </BODY>.

This should leave us with the following, which is the basic structure or template for every HTML document (with a different title, of course):

```
<HTML>
<HEAD>
<TITLE>Bill's Home Page</TITLE>
</HEAD>
<BODY>
</BODY>
</HTML>
```

Everything else we create will go between the two BODY tags and will be what is displayed in the Web browser. Everyone have what I have?

SAVE AND VIEW

Before we go on we need to save what we've done. As with all documents you create, you should save frequently.

I am passing out floppy disks; everyone please take one.

[Pass out floppy disks.]

This will be your disk, where you will save the document you are creating today; you will continue to work on this document throughout the series, so you need to hang on to this disk and bring it with you to every session.

OK, insert the disk into the drive.

[As always, do this on your machine as well, so that everyone can follow along.]

Next, in Notepad, with your HTML document open, choose File in the menu at the top, and then Save As. Go to the Floppy (A) drive in the Save In box at the top. At the bottom, in the Save As Type box, choose All Files, if it is not that already. Then, in the File Name box above that, give the file a name. I am going to call mine "Bill's Home Page.html." Give yours a similar name, and please remember to type the .html extension.

[If the operating system you are using does not support long file names and extensions, modify as necessary.]

That should do it. Everyone got that saved on your floppy?

Next, I want us to look at what we have created in our browser. Bring your browser up on the screen; you should still have it open and just need to click it from the bottom bar of programs you have open.

In the browser, we are going to open up and display our local HTML file. In the browser menu at the top, choose File, then Open. Click the Browse button, and then find your A: drive. (It should be under My Computer.) Open that, and you should see your one HTML file you saved. Double-click on that to open it, or click it once and then click the Open button. Then click OK. What do you get?

[Get responses.]

Yes, a blank screen. That's because we haven't put anything in the body of our document yet. But notice the title bar at the top of the browser window. Do you all see the title you gave your document? This should be what we put between the TITLE tags. Mine says "Bill's Home Page." Does everyone have his or her title there?

OK, we're all set to start putting stuff in the body of our document!

Other Structural and Presentation Tags (0:30–0:40)

HEADING

Let's all click back to our HTML document in Notepad. Insert your cursor after the initial BODY tag. You might want to insert a carriage return or two, just so we have some room and can see better. I will do that now, too.

First, let's give our document a big heading that will be displayed at the top of our page. HTML has six heading levels, 1 through 6, and 1 is the largest. We want the one at the top to be our biggest heading, so let's make it a level 1 heading.

Everyone type with me the tag <H1>. That's the opening heading level 1 tag.

Next, we will to type the text that will be affected by this tag. This is often the same text as the title, since this top heading kind of functions as a title, too. Let's use that same text again. Next to the opening heading tag <H1>, I am going to type in *Bill's Home Page.* You type in your similar text, using your own name.

Then, we need an end tag. Like the others we've done, this will be the same as the start tag, except it will have the backslash. So the end heading tag is </H1>. Type that in and click File/Save to save your changes.

Now let's look at that in our browser. Let's open our browsers again (click on it on the bottom bar). You should still have the same page as before—the blank screen, with just the title in the title bar at the top. If you click the Refresh button in your browser, what happens?

[Get responses.]

Yes, the heading we just created is now displayed. Does everyone have that?

So, you see, a level one heading displays the text very big and in bold. Levels two to six get progressively smaller. We'll take a look at some of those levels before we're done.

PARAGRAPH

Let's go back to our HTML document in Notepad. Now I want us to type in some text about ourselves. As I mentioned before, carriage returns in HTML have no effect, so the way to define some chunks of text and create some space on the Web page is to use the <P> tag, which stands for paragraph. In our HTML document, I want you to insert your cursor after the closing heading tag </H1> we just created. Do a couple of carriage returns to give yourself some room, and then type the opening paragraph tag, which is like this: <P>. This indicates to the browser that a new paragraph is starting. Immediately after the opening paragraph tag, I want you to write two or three sentences about yourself: for instance, where you grew up, perhaps where you have lived and gone to school, maybe something about your family. For example, I am going to write:

[Do this in your HTML document, and have everyone watch.]

<P>I was born and raised in Miami, Florida, and grew up in a large family. I have been to school in Massachusetts, Michigan, and England, and have lived in a number of places, including New York City. Currently, I live in Seattle, Washington.</P>

You'll notice that I did some carriage returns; I only did that because Notepad does not automatically wrap text and I want to be able to see all the text on one screen. These carriage returns will have no effect whatsoever in the HTML document, so you can insert them wherever you want. You don't have to insert them at all, but I suggest that you do so that you can see all your text on one screen without having to scroll to the right and left.

Don't worry about what you write; you can always go back and change it, and we aren't going to post these pages—at least not yet! We just need some text to work with. Don't write about work, though; we are going to save that for the next paragraph.

OK, let's take a minute and write our two to three sentences.

[You may want to walk around in case people have questions or are stuck.]

Everybody finished? Does everyone have something that looks somewhat like what I have here, with the opening paragraph tag (<P>), some text, and then the closing paragraph tag (</P>)?

Now let's write a second paragraph—again, just two to three sentences—this time about your work. You could write about your work history, about your current job, or a little of both. For example, I am going to insert my opening paragraph tag <P>, and then I am going to write:

[Do this in your HTML document, and have everyone watch.]

<P>I worked for 4 years at the New York Public Library, where I worked both for the Research Libraries and for the Branch Libraries. While I was at NYPL, my jobs focused on training and on the Internet. I also provided reference services in the business division of the Research Library.</P>

Notice that I included both my start and end paragraph tags. Again, don't worry too much about what you write. We just need some more text, and you can revise it later.

OK, let's take a minute and write our two to three sentences.

[You may want to walk around in case people have questions or are stuck.]

Everybody done? Anybody stuck?

Let's take a look at what we have done. First save your changes in Notepad . . .

[Demonstrate File/Save again and have everyone do it on their machines]

. . . and then click to open your browser. Your previous page should still be open. Click the Refresh button. Do you all have the two paragraphs you just wrote displaying properly?

So the start and end paragraph tags are what define the chunks of text between them; they create the white space above and below. I can do any number of carriage returns in my HTML document . . .

[Demonstrate on your machine. Do five or more quick carriage returns in the middle of one of the paragraphs, save it, and then refresh your browser.]

. . . and it makes absolutely no difference in the browser display. Similarly, I could add a bunch of spaces

[Go back to the HTML document and add five or more spaces between two words, save it, and then refresh your browser.]

. . . and, again, it does not make any difference in the browser display. It only inserts one space. Rather, it is the tags themselves that define the structure and the display.

By the way, the ending paragraph tag is actually optional, but it is good HTML practice to include it. Also, having it will allow us to do some fancier stuff, like align the paragraph on the page, which you will learn about later. So it's a good idea just to get in the habit of including that ending paragraph tag </P> now.

Are there any questions at this point?

LINE BREAK

You'll notice that the paragraph tag inserts a space between the paragraphs. But sometimes you might want to just have text start on a new line, without any additional space. For example, if you were going to type an address, it might look weird to have extra spaces between the lines. In a case such as this, you would use the <BR> tag—BR for break, or link break.

[Demonstrate below.]

For example, I am going to write my contact information:

<P>Here is my contact information:</P>
123 Main Street
Anytown, USA 12345
222-333-4444

Notice that, for the address and telephone part, I only have to put the break tag <BR> at the end of the line. This is an example of a tag that does not come in pairs. Let's take a look at what I have done. I will save this, open my browser, and hit refresh.

[Save the changes to the HTML document, and then refresh your browser.]

You see it creates line breaks for me—carriage returns, if you will—but without the extra space that a paragraph tag creates.

Now I want you all to type in your contact information, similar to what I have done, but using your own contact information, of course. You can use personal or work address and phone, or you can make it up. Doesn't matter.

[You may want to walk around in case people have questions or are stuck.]

After you're finished, save your changes in the HTML document, and then refresh your browser to see if it worked.

[Continue to walk around and offer assistance, if necessary.]

Everybody all set?

HORIZONTAL RULE

Let's insert a horizontal line in our document. This is done with the HR tag, which stands for horizontal rule. Let's put it after the second paragraph and before the "Here is my contact information" part. The HR tag is another one that doesn't need a closing tag, since it doesn't enclose any text.

[Insert in your document to demonstrate.]

And let's save that and take a look at it in our browser. As you see, this line can be inserted to break up your document at logical points and create a more attractive design. Don't overuse it, though! In general, with Web pages, the simpler the better. And the more white space the better.

So now we have learned how to create the basic structure for a Web page: the HTML document type, the head, the body, the title. We have also learned how to create some other fundamental structural and presentation tags for text within the body of the document: headers, paragraphs, line breaks, and horizontal rules. Now I want to turn to a few more tags that relate to text formatting.

Here is a recap of what I have done so far. Does everyone have something that looks like this?

```
<HTML>
<HEAD>
<TITLE>Bill's Home Page</TITLE>
</HEAD>
<BODY>
<H1>Bill's Home Page</H1>
<P>I was born and raised in Miami, Florida, and grew up in a large
family. I have been to school in Massachusetts, Michigan, and England,
and have lived in a number of places, including New York City. Cur-
rently, I live in Seattle, Washington.</P>
<P>I worked for 4 years at the New York Public Library, where I worked
both for the Research Libraries and for the Branch Libraries. While I
was at NYPL, my jobs focused on training and on the Internet. I also
provided reference services in the business division of the Research Li-
brary.</P>
<HR>
<P>Here is my contact information:</P>
123 Main Street<BR>
Anytown, USA 12345<BR>
222-333-4444<BR>
</BODY>
</HTML>
```

Text Formatting (0:40–0:50)

BOLD

Let's make something bold; in my example, I am going to put the New York Public Library in bold. The start tag for bold is <B> and the end tag is </B>. I will put the start tag before the text I want bold, and the end tag at the end of the text I want bold. I will do that now. All of you pick something—a word or two—to put in bold, and do the same. Choose something in your first two paragraphs, not in your contact information.

[Do it on your machine, so everyone can refer to what you are doing.]

ITALICS

Next, let's say we want to put "Here is my contact information:" in italics. The tags for that are <I> and </I>. Can anyone tell me where I should put those?

[Get responses.]

Usually, you'll want to put the formatting tag inside the structural tag. So type the start <I> tag before the word "Here," and after "information:" type the end </I> tag. When you do something like this—putting tags within other tags—be careful about making them symmetrical. Just as our two TITLE tags are both within our two HEAD tags, for instance, so the two italics tags surround all of the text, and these are in turn surrounded by the paragraph tags.

Let's all insert our italics tags, save our changes, refresh our browsers, and take a look.

[Demonstrate.]

Does everyone have the bold and the italics showing up properly in the Web page?

FONT: SIZE

So we have put some text in bold, and some in italics. But it's still a bit boring. Is there anything else we can do with the font? Well, yes. We can change its size, its color, and even its type. This is done by using the FONT tag.

Let's take size first. I'll demonstrate on my document.

[Demonstrate.]

Let's say that in my first sentence ("I was born and raised in Miami, Florida, and grew up in a large family.") I want to put the word "large" in a bigger font for emphasis. I would surround it with the FONT tag and also give it a SIZE attribute. The size can range from 1 to 7; size 3 is usually the base or default font. If I want a size 5 font, I can either specify 5, or specify +2 (since 3 is the default, adding 3+2 equals 5). It really doesn't matter which method you choose, but I tend to use relative sizes (the plus and minus signs) because there is also a way to change the base font from something other than 3, if we want to. If we did do that, then all the relative size changes would still be in effect.

So I am going to tag it <FONT SIZE="+2">large</FONT>.

Let's take a look at that in the browser.

[Continue to demonstrate.]

And, obviously, I could make the font size smaller by using the minus sign (–1 or –2), to go down to font size 1.

FONT: COLOR

Now I want to give the word "large" some pizzazz by putting it in another color—say, green. I will do that by adding the COLOR attribute of the FONT tag, like this:

[Demonstrate.]

<FONT SIZE="+2" COLOR=GREEN>large</FONT>

And, I will save this and take a look in my browser.

[Continue to demonstrate.]

We will talk more about text and background color in our third session.

FONT: FACE

Finally, let's say I decide I don't like this default font type, and I want to put my entire document in another font. Then, you use the FACE attribute of the FONT tag. I am going to insert this around all of the text I have in the BODY of the document. So, my final document today looks like this:

```
<HTML>
<HEAD>
<TITLE>Bill's Home Page</TITLE>
</HEAD>
<BODY>
<FONT FACE="Arial,Helvetica">
<H1>Bill's Home Page</H1>
<P>I was born and raised in Miami, Florida, and grew up in a <FONT
SIZE="+2" COLOR=GREEN>large</FONT> family. I have been to
```

school in Massachusetts, Michigan, and England, and have lived in a number of places, including New York City. Currently, I live in Seattle, Washington.</P>
<P>I worked for 4 years at <B>the New York Public Library</B>, where I worked both for the Research Libraries and for the Branch Libraries. While I was at NYPL, my jobs focused on training and on the Internet. I also provided reference services in the business division of the Research Library.</P>
<HR>
<P><I>Here is my contact information:</I><P>
123 Main Street
Anytown, USA 12345
222-333-4444
</FONT>
</BODY>
</HTML>

Notice that I listed more than one FONT style. This is the list of fonts in preferential order. If the Web browser that someone is using doesn't support the first choice, it will move on to the second, and so on.

Logical Tags

The text formatting tags we have just covered are examples of what some people call *physical tags*. Physical tags tell the browser how to display the text. But there are also what are sometimes called *logical tags* which also affect how text is displayed. The difference is that logical tags only tell the browser to emphasize a piece of text in some way, and leaves it up to individual browsers how to do that (by putting it in italics or bold, for instance). For example, there is a tag <EM> for emphasis that is usually displayed as italics, a tag <STRONG> for strong emphasis that is usually displayed in bold, and a tag <CITE> for citation that is usually displayed as italics.

Some people prefer physical tags, some people prefer logical. It doesn't really matter which type of tag you choose, although you should usually stick with one type of tag or the other throughout the document.

Assignment: Lists (0:50–0:55)

Lists: Unordered, Ordered, Definition

Finally, you have homework! It's impossible to learn everything you need to know—all of the tags you will need—during training sessions. A lot of HTML and Web creation involves research—research on your own, finding out how to do something. Usually, the best place to do this is to go online, and I am going to give you some starting points.

And so your assignment involves research. I want you to add to your HTML document that you have created today, and what I want you to add are three different kinds of *lists*.

[Have these written on a board or flip chart ahead of time.]

First, I want you to create an *unordered* list of three of your favorite foods.

Second, I want you to create an *ordered* (or numbered) list of your three favorite movies of all time.

Finally, I want you to create a *definition* list of three Web sites that you like, with a short (one- or two-sentence) annotation for each.

Just add these lists to the end of your document, save it on your floppy disk, and bring it with you to the next class.

Handout (pages 203–206)

There are many places to learn the tags to create these lists, and a number are listed on the handout I am passing around right now. As I said, usually the best place to learn about HTML and Web development is on the Internet itself, but I've also included a few books and magazines.

I want to point out a few sites that will be helpful for your assignment. The Introduction to HTML (*http://www.cwru.edu/help/introHTML/toc.html*) and the NCSA Beginner's Guide to HTML (*http://www.ncsa.uiuc.edu/General/ Internet/WWW/HTMLPrimer.html*) are excellent introductions to HTML and will have information on how to create these three types of lists; I would start with those. And The Bare Bones Guide to HTML (*http://werbach.com/ barebones/*) and Rob Schluter's HTML Tag List (*http://utopia.knoware.nl/ users/schluter/doc/tags/*) can be useful as quick references to HTML tags.

Review and Wrap Up (0:55–1:00)

Copy Document to Hard Drive/Reminder to Bring Back Floppy

Before we go today, I want each of you to copy the HTML document you have created to the hard drive of your computer.

[Do this yourself as well, so that everyone can follow along with you.]

Click on the Windows Start button in the lower left corner, choose Programs, then choose Windows Explorer. Select the A: drive. Select your HTML document (mine is Bill's Home Page.html) and then drag it over to the hard C: drive and release, so that it will copy it to the hard drive.

[Instead of the parent directory, copy to a subdirectory on the hard drive if that makes sense.]

Once you have copied the file, exit out of Windows Explorer by clicking on the X in the upper right corner, or choosing File/Close.

This way, we have a copy in case you lose your floppy or forget to bring it. But please, please, please don't lose it, and please remember to bring it with you next time. It will make things much easier.

REVIEW

We have covered a lot of ground today. We learned that HTML is a set of tags that tell the World Wide Web browser how to display a document. We learned that there are a number of tools that you can use to create HTML documents, from a simple text editor to word processors to WYSIWYG HTML editors. And we created an HTML document. First we gave it a basic structure, with the HTML, HEAD, TITLE, and BODY tags. And then we worked on formatting text—including tags for headings, paragraphs, line breaks, horizontal rules, bold, italics, and font styles. And we learned that, in addition to physical tags, you can also use logical tags to structure and format text. That's a lot!

See you next time!

9

Introduction to HTML (Part 2): Links and Troubleshooting

Handouts for this workshop follow page 197.

OVERVIEW

Who

This second in the series of HTML training workshops is designed for trainees who have already taken "Introduction to HTML (Part 1): Structure and Text." Preferably the same group of people will go through this training series together, but it is not necessary.

What

This is a series of three hands-on workshops providing a basic introduction to HTML. Part 2 introduces linking (internal, external, absolute, relative, and e-mail); it also offers troubleshooting advice and tips.

Where

Like Part 1, this training session is designed for a computer lab with space for ten students and an instructor (11 PCs total). The instructor's PC has projection. Each of the computers has Internet access, Microsoft Internet Explorer (or another graphical browser), Windows 95 or Windows 98 (this workshop can be adapted easily to another operating system), and Notepad (or another plain text editor).

When

This session should take place soon after Part 1, but allowing enough time for everyone to complete the assignment. One week is ideal. This session lasts one hour.

Why

The objectives of this three-part series are for the trainees to be able to (1) explain the concepts of HTML; (2) create basic Web pages using correct HTML (text, links, and graphics); and (3) use appropriate resources effectively for further learning and reference.

The objectives for Part 2 are for the trainees to be able to (1) explain the concept of linking; (2) execute a variety of links in HTML (internal, external, absolute, relative, and e-mail); and (3) use effective HTML troubleshooting techniques.

WORKSHOP AGENDA

Again, this agenda moves quickly into hands-on HTML work; therefore, it would help (although it's not necessary) to have an assistant, who can aid anyone who gets stuck and falls behind. Linking can be exciting for the participants to learn, but it requires everyone to be comfortable with files and directory structure.

Assignment Review: Lists (0:00–0:07)

- Demonstration of Lists
- Objectives for this Session

ABSOLUTE LINKS (0:10–0:20)

- Hotlinks
- Providing exact path

RELATIVE LINKS (0:20–0:30)

- Link to another document in same directory
- Link to another document in same subdirectory

INTERNAL LINKS (0:30–0:40)

- Link to another part in same document
- Advantages of internal links

MAIL LINKS (0:40–0:45)

- Mailto reference

TROUBLESHOOTING (0:45–0:50)

- All upper- or lowercase
- Each command on new line
- Files saved and checked regularly
- Things to watch for

ASSIGNMENTS (0:50–1:00)

- Assignment #1: Links
- Assignment #2: Images
- Copy to Hard Drive/Reminder to Bring Back Disk

REVIEW

SAMPLE SCRIPT

This sample script follows the lesson plan above. Just be clear about when the trainees should work on their machines, and when they should just watch and listen to you.

Again, this session assumes that you are using Internet Explorer, Windows 95 or Windows 98, and Notepad.

Assignment Review: Lists (0:00–0:07)

Welcome back! How did the assignment go? Did everyone learn how to make the three lists?

Who would like to volunteer to come up with your floppy disk and show us on the projector what you came up with?

[Have a volunteer come up and show the class his or her unordered, ordered, and definition lists. Go over each tag set—<UL>, <OL>, <DL>, etc. If there are any problems in the markup, ask the class how they might be fixed.]

Thank you so much for sharing your lists! Excellent job!
I'll show you my lists quickly, too.

[The following is optional. It might be useful as a reinforcement to go through the list tags again, but if you feel they were covered clearly in the volunteer's demonstration, you can eliminate your own demonstration.]

Here is what I came up with:

[Project your lists and talk through the list tags; this is a sample of what yours—and everyone's—might look like.]

```
<P>Here are three of my favorite foods:</P>
<UL>
<LI>Pepperoni Pizza
<LI>Chocolate Cake
<LI>Green Beans
</UL>
<P>These are three of my favorite movies:</P>
<OL>
<LI>The Godfather
<LI>Double Indemnity
<LI>The Wizard of Oz
</OL>
```

```
<P>Here are three Web sites I like:</P>
<DL>
<DT>The Library of Congress
<DD>The Library of Congress has some terrific exhibits up on the Web,
plus their catalog is searchable.
<DT>The Internet Movie Database
<DD>This site is great for movie trivia; it lists credits for just about ev-
ery movie you could think of, is fully searchable, and offers links to
other resources.
<DT>The American Kennel Club
<DD>This organization provides extensive information about many dif-
ferent kinds of dog breeds; the pictures are great, too.
</DL>
```

Are there questions about any of these kinds of lists?

Objectives for This Session (0:07–0:10)

Now we have the basics for structure and text in HTML. Today we are going to focus on links, and also on troubleshooting. We have three objectives for this session.

[Have these already written on a board or flip chart.]

At the end of this hour, you will be able to

(1) explain the concept of linking;
(2) execute a variety of links in HTML (internal, external, absolute, relative, and e-mail); and
(3) use effective HTML troubleshooting techniques.

Linking is the heart of HTML. After all, HTML stands for Hypertext Markup Language, and linking is what hypertext is all about—being able to jump from document to document, file to file. So let's get started!

Absolute Links (0:10–0:20)

Before we begin, everyone please insert your disk, start up Notepad, and open the HTML file you have been working on.

[If any students neglected to bring back their disks, they will have to use the same PC as they used for Part 1 so they can open the documents they copied onto the hard drive.]

I want everyone to type this sentence with me at the end of your HTML document.

[Demonstrate on the projector as you do it.]

<P>Yahoo is a directory of Internet resources.</P>

Now, let's say we want to create a hot link (also called hyperlink or simply link) on the word Yahoo, and have it actually link to the Yahoo site. Well, the way to do that is to type the following, around the word Yahoo. Everyone do this along with me.

<P><A HREF="http://www.yahoo.com/">Yahoo</A> is a directory of Internet resources.</P>

Does everyone have that?

Let's go over what this is. The main tag for linking is the <A> anchor tag. Within the anchor tag, the HREF parameter specifies where to go—in this case, the URL for Yahoo. The text—the actual word or words, in this case the word Yahoo—is what will be highlighted; that will be the hypertext link. The closing </A> anchor tag marks the end of the text you want to serve as the link.

Let's save that and take a look in our browser. Remember, in Notepad, do File, then Save. Then go to your browser (open it if it isn't open already). In the browser menu at the top, choose File, then Open. Click the Browse button, and then find your Floppy (A) drive. (It should be under My Computer.) Open that, and you should see the HTML file you saved. Double-click on that to open it, or click it once and then click the Open button. Then click OK.

Does everyone have Yahoo as a hot link? Try it and see if it works.

Did everyone get to the Yahoo site from the link you just created?

[A few people are likely to have made some errors in their HTML. Spend one or two minutes helping these folks.]

Now let's go back to our HTML documents and create another link. Let's add a link to the library's home page.

[Use your library's home page, if available. We will use the Seattle Public Library as our example. Continue to demonstrate, as the others also do it themselves.]

Everyone type the following sentence.

<P>My job at the library keeps me very busy.</P>

Now, let's make the word "library" hot, that is, code it so we can click on it to link to another page. So we have:

<P>My job at the <A HREF="http://www.spl.lib.wa.us/">library</A> keeps me very busy.</P>

Now let's save this, open our browser, hit the Refresh button, and take a look.

Did that work for everyone?

So, you see, the actual text that is hot can be anything, although you will usually want it to make sense and tell the user (or at least imply) where the link will take him or her. And, in fact, the link does not have to be text at all; it can be an image. But we'll save images until the next session.

Does anyone have any questions so far about creating links?

Relative Links (0:20–0:30)

We have been creating what are called "absolute links." This means that we have told the browser the exact path to take to find the specified file. In other words, we gave the entire URL—for example, *http://www.yahoo.com/*.

But you don't always have to specify the entire path. Sometimes, you can just tell the browser where to look relative to where you are—in other words, relative to where the HTML document you are linking from resides. These are called "relative links." When we do an example, this will become clearer.

First, though, we need quickly to create another HTML document on our floppy diskettes. I want you to go back to Notepad, save your current HTML document (don't forget to do this!), and then select File/New.

This brings up a new Notepad window. I want us to recreate our basic HTML document structure—with the HTML, HEAD, and BODY tags—and give our new document a title called . . .

[Write these two text items on a white board or flip chart.]

. . . "A Second Page" and with body text consisting only of "Here is a second HTML page I have created."

I'll create mine along with you, and you can watch me as I do it.

[Everyone creates his or her second page.]

This is what everyone should have. Does everyone have this?

```
<HTML>
<HEAD>
<TITLE>A Second Page</TITLE>
</HEAD>
<BODY>
Here is a second HTML page I have created.
</BODY>
</HTML>
```

OK, now please save this new HTML document on your floppy drive, and call it "second.html." Remember, in Notepad choose File in the menu at the top, and then Save As. Go to the A: drive in the Save In box at the top. At the bottom, in the Save As Type box, choose All Files, if it is not that already. Then, in the File Name box above that, call the file "second.html." Remember to type the .html extension!

Let's take a look at this second file in the browser window, just to make sure everything is OK with it. As always, in the browser menu at the top, choose File, then Open. Click the Browse button, and then find your A: drive. Open that, and you should see the file "second.html" that you just created. Double-click on that to open it, or click it once and then click the Open button. Then click OK.

Did everyone's new document, which should just read "Here is a second HTML page I have created," come up OK?

Now, we want to create a link from our original HTML document to this second document. Let's go back to Notepad, close this "second.html" and open our original HTML documents.

Everyone got those open?

OK, now I want everyone to add the following sentence to the end of your document:

[Demonstrate.]

```
<P>Here is a link to another document I have created.</P>
```

Has everyone added that sentence?

Now, let's create a link from the words "another document" to the second document we just created. So this is how we would do that.

[Continue to demonstrate.]

```
<P>Here is a link to <A HREF="second.html">another document</A>
I have created.</P>
```

The thing to notice here is that I haven't typed an entire pathname for the destination. I have only typed the name of the file—"second.html." This is because the two files—the one I am linking from and the one I am linking to—live in this same place; they are both on the A: drive, in the same directory. Therefore, you don't have to type the entire path to find the new file; if you just type the file name, it assumes to look in the same directory. What we did was create a relative link, not an absolute link. We specified where to look for the new file *relative* to the location of the file we are linking from.

Has everyone done this in their documents? Let's take a look in our browsers. Open your browser, and then open your original HTML file. Does everyone have the link? Now check to see if it jumps to the second file you created. Did it work for everyone?

[Answer questions and deal with any problems for a minute or two.]

So that is basically how a relative link works. And, to have this continue to work, I'll have to keep these files in the same directory no matter where they go. For instance, if I actually load these files onto a Web server so that others can access them, these files will have to travel together and stay in the same directory. If I move them into different locations (into different directories), I'll have to alter the relative link I created to find the new location, or maybe create an absolute link. We'll talk a little more about uploading to servers in a later class.

We created a relative link to a document in the same directory as the original document, and so we just needed to type the file name. But you can also create relative links to documents that are in different directories but on the same server and in the same directory structure. Here's how you would do that:

[Diagram this structure on a board or flip chart.]

The syntax for the parent directory is "..". So, for example, let's say I have a directory on the server called "Bill" with two subdirectories, one called "classes" and the other called "guides." I want to create a link from a document in the "classes" subdirectory to a document (let's call it "sports.html") in the "guides" subdirectory. I would create the link as follows:

[Write this on the board or flip chart.]

<A HREF="../guides/sports.html">Guide to Sports Resources</A>

This example contains the path from the parent directory, Bill (the ".."), to the correct subdirectory ("guides") to the correct file name ("sports.html"). If you were pointing to a file within a subdirectory of the directory you are already in, you could eliminate the ".." because you wouldn't have to return to the parent directory.

I know this is a little confusing, but the more you work with it the clearer it gets. The important thing to remember is that relative links are useful because, as long as you keep the same basic structure, you can move files around and the links will still work. You can create a bunch of HTML files and put them in the same directory or folder, and then move the entire folder onto the server. Files with relative links become easier to move around. They are also more efficient in terms of server usage. And there is less to type!

One thing to remember is case sensitivity. DOS-based systems are not case sensitive, but UNIX is. So if you are uploading to a UNIX server, you need to make sure your file names in your relative links are correct in terms of case. Even though it may work in DOS if the cases don't match, it's always a good idea to have them match anyway, just to save headaches down the road.

So relative links are really useful for documents that you control, because they are more portable and they are more efficient in terms of server connection. But absolute links are still important to use for links to documents that you don't control, and whose relative location to your documents might change—for instance, links to another library department's Web pages. Also, of course, you will continue to use absolute links to point to totally external URLs—like the link to Yahoo, for instance.

That brings up another point. Always remember that other people may be linking to your documents. At least, that is what you hope! Therefore, it's a good idea not to move your files around too much, because you want their links to work, and not everyone is always good about checking the links on their Web pages. Only move files around when it's really necessary. And, if you do move a file, consider putting up a notice that the file has moved, and offering a link to the new location, at least temporarily. That's often called a "redirect," and it helps keep Web traffic moving.

Internal Links (0:30–0:40)

We have learned how to create links to external documents and files, using both absolute links and relative links. But it's also possible to create links to other sections within a document itself. You have, I'm sure, seen this on Web pages: a kind of "table of contents" at the beginning of a Web page that takes you, if you click on one of the links, lower down on the document to the specific section you wanted. Let's learn how to create an internal link like this.

First, right under our heading at the top of our document (mine says "Bill's Home Page"), let's put in the text that we want to link from. Let's say we want to add a link to the section of our document that lists our favorite foods. Let's all type . . .

[Demonstrate.]

<P>Favorite Food</P>

Everyone got that? Now we need to make that a link. So we will use the same tags for linking we have been learning about—the anchor tag <A>, and the HREF parameter for the reference. But what is our reference? It's not an absolute link (not a URL), and it's not the name of a separate file.

Well, we're going to give it a name. This will be our "named anchor" and the named anchor will be where we jump to. Let's call it "Food." And this is how we code it.

[Demonstrate.]

<P><A HREF="#Food">Favorite Food</A></P>

Notice, in the quotation marks, the reference is to our named anchor "Food"; the hash mark (#) is the convention that says, basically, "look for this place within the document to go to." It's like a tab mark within the document.

Have you all added this link in your document?

Now we have to create the named anchor itself. We want the link to jump to the beginning of our list of favorite foods. I have a sentence at the beginning that reads "Here are three of my favorite foods," so I am going to put my anchor there. And this is how I do it.

<P><A NAME="Food">Here are three of my favorite foods:</A></P>

Instead of the HREF parameter, we used the NAME parameter, which tells the browser that this is a named anchor. And the text in quotation marks has to match the text I put after the hash mark as my link reference.

I am going to save this and check to see if this worked in my browser.

[Demonstrate.]

So, you see, this inserted the link at the top, and the link jumps to the section of the document named as the anchor.

Now, everyone insert your named anchor somewhere at the beginning of your Favorite Food list, save it, and check to see if it worked in your browser.

[Walk around and help anyone who is stuck or has questions.]

Has that worked for everyone?

Let's do one more. Underneath the link we just created at the top of the page, let's create one to link to the three Web sites we included in our definition list. Let's do that one now.

[Do yours along with everyone, so that they can refer to what you are doing.]

My link looks like this: <P><A HREF="#Web Sites">Web Sites I Like</A></P>. And my named anchor looks like this: <P><A NAME="Web Sites">Here are three Web sites I like:</A></P>

Does everyone have that? Let's check it out in our browsers to see if it worked. Don't forget to save the changes to your HTML file in Notepad, and then refresh your browsers!

[Do this along with everyone else.]

Did that work for everyone? For some of you, you may have noticed that the jump—especially for the Web sites list—may not have brought the named anchor all the way to the top of the screen. That's because there wasn't enough text below it to fill up an entire screen, and so it just goes as far as it can go.

So now we have learned to create internal links. Why would you want to use internal links like this?

[Get responses.]

Yes, internal links are useful if you have a long document and you don't want to make the user scroll down to find the particular section they are interested in. Our document isn't really long enough for these kinds of links to make sense, but you get the idea.

I just wanted to mention that, if you do have a very long document, you'll have to decide whether or not it makes sense to divide it into actual separate documents, or leave it as one long document. Very long documents can take a long time to load for the user, particularly if there are a lot of images and graphics, so breaking it up into separate files will make sense sometimes. But there are also advantages to leaving a document as one file. It may take longer to load, but once it does, the entire document is right there, and the user doesn't have to click on a link to open a separate file to go to another section. Also, if it is the kind of document that you imagine people will want to print, it makes sense to leave it as one long file to making printing easier.

So there are advantages and disadvantages to each; sometimes you'll want to break up long documents into separate files, and sometimes you'll want to leave them together. If you do leave a long document intact, though, be sure to include a table of contents at the beginning, with internal links like we have just learned about; that way, the user can navigate the long document more easily and jump right to the section that he or she is interested in.

By the way, you can also link to specific sections of other documents, but only if they already have named anchors in the HTML coding, or if you have access to the code and can change it. Remember that you can select View Source on any document, which will allow you to see if the author has included anchor tags on the page.

E-mail Links (0:40–0:45)

Finally, let's create an e-mail link. We have all seen on Web sites how there is often an e-mail address link—maybe to the Webmaster or to the person who is the author of the page. You can click on that link, and up pops a mail window and you can send that person an e-mail message. It's really easy to create such a link; let's learn how to do that now.

First, let's add our e-mail address to our list of contact information near the top of our document. Again, you can either use your real e-mail address, or make one up. After my telephone number, I am going to type:

[Demonstrate.]

bill@myprovider.com

Does everyone have an e-mail address typed? Now let's make the address hot. We do this in the same way as any link, except that the reference is going to be a "mailto" one. Here's what it looks like:

<A HREF="mailto:bill@myprovider.com">bill@myprovider.com</A>

So, like any link, it has the <A> anchor tags at the beginning and the end. The reference in the quotation marks, though, includes "mailto," which indicates that this is a mail link, and then the e-mail address itself. Note that the syntax here is mailto, a colon, and the address, without a space in between any of the elements.

Go ahead and add your link, save your changes, and then check it out in your browser.

[Walk around and help anyone who is stuck or has questions.]

How did that work for everybody? Having a mail link allows users of a Web page to communicate with the author. Often, users will point out errors in the page that you may not have noticed, or will offer suggestions on how to improve or add to the page.

Troubleshooting (0:45–0:50)

Speaking of errors, I want to talk for a few minutes about HTML troubleshooting tips. We have learned a lot of tags over the last two sessions, and you will continue to learn even more in the next training session and in the future. The HTML markup gets increasingly long and complicated, and it's easy to make errors. And one little tag element that is off or missing can affect the entire document.

So it's important to be able to troubleshoot your document. A lot of this will involve being able to scan your HTML document quickly and easily for errors.

[Write the main points below on a board or flip chart.]

I have already mentioned one way to make this easier: for your HTML tags, *use either all upper or all lower case.* This consistency will make scanning easier on the eye; you will be able to pick out the tags easier. As I said, I tend to prefer all upper case; I think it makes the tags stand out even more.

I also already mentioned another technique that helps in this way: in your HTML document, *put all new tags and new elements on new lines.* There is nothing worse than trying to pick out where an HTML error is when all of the text and tags are strung along together. In the HTML document, it doesn't matter where the spaces and carriage returns are, so why not make it easy on yourself? Put them all on new lines, and even put in some extra spaces to make the document easier for the eye to scan.

Save and check your HTML files regularly. Don't wait until you have created an entire document to check how it looks in the browser. If you save and check your changes regularly, it will be easier to catch and isolate a problem quickly.

As you are scanning your HTML document for a mistake, watch out for certain things that can throw your entire document off:

- A *missing angle (< or >) bracket,* often the closing right angle bracket, may be the problem. Also, watch out for extra, stray angle brackets.
- Similarly, you might be *missing the entire closing tag.* For example, you have the initial <B> tag for bold, but are missing the closing </B> tag, in which case the rest of your document is in bold.

- Look out for *spelling errors* in your codes and in the file names you are linking to (and, of course, in your entire document). You might want to use a spell-check program.
- Watch out for *asymmetrical (or overlapping) tags*. You want to make sure that your nesting of codes is symmetrical. For example, <B><I>text</I></B> is correct; <B><I>text</B></I> is not. Sometimes asymmetrical nesting will cause problems, and sometimes it won't. It's better just to keep everything symmetrical.

Consider using an HTML validation service. Two examples on your hand-out are Web Site Garage and WebTechs Validation Service. These services will tell you if your code conforms to accepted HTML specifications, and they will also do things like check your links.

Check your page on different browsers and monitors. All pages look a little different depending on the browser and the monitor, so check how your page looks on a few different ones, if you can. And, by all means, since you can't check every browser and every monitor, the safest thing to do is to conform to standard HTML specifications.

Finally, keep your documents up-to-date. If your page only has static, historical information—such as a biography of an historical figure—this may not be so important. But most pages you create will contain links and timely information, and there is nothing worse than going to someone's page where all the links are broken, and the last update was done two years ago.

Assignments (0:50–1:00)

ASSIGNMENT #1: LINKS

OK, you have two assignments to complete before our next session, but they are both quick and easy. First, I want everyone to add links to the three Web sites you included in your definition list. Use what we learned today, and make the titles hot, so that they jump to the sites listed.

Any questions on that assignment?

ASSIGNMENT #2: IMAGES

Your second assignment is to come back next time with an image or a graphic saved on your diskette that you want to use in your HTML document. The next session focuses on graphics and color, so everyone needs an image to work with.

It's easy to find a graphic. On your handout, I have listed five clip art sites, where you can freely save and use any one of thousands of images. Two of these sites focus on graphics related to libraries, such as books and computers. These sites are the Library Clipart Collection (*http://www.netins.net/showcase/meyers/library_clipart/clipart.html*) and Library Graphics (*http://www.geocities.com/Athens/Acropolis/2161/clipart/index.htm*). The other three clip art resources on your handout include graphics related to all kinds of subjects: Barry's Clip Art Server (*http://www.barrysclipart.com/*), Clip Art Review (*http://www.webplaces.com/html/clipart.htm*), and Cool Graphics (*http://www.fishnet.net/~gini/cool/*). Most of you already know this, but "clip art" is shorthand for an image that is free of copyright restrictions, meaning it can be freely used in new documents. Beware of otherwise copying artwork off the Net and pasting it into your own documents without getting permission; you could get yourself, or your library, into trouble!

I want you to browse around some of these sites, find a graphic you like, save it to your floppy (the same floppy that includes the HTML document you have been creating), and bring it with you next week. Let me show you quickly how easy that is to do.

> [Demonstrate the following. Choose any graphic and clip art site you like, and make the necessary adjustments to the script.]

I am going to the Library Graphics (*http://www.geocities.com/Athens/Acropolis/2161/clipart/index.htm*) page. If I scroll down, you'll notice they have lots of different kinds of graphics. Under Books I am going to choose Medium. This brings up another page with a lot of book images. I like the one of three books tied together with a leather strap. On my mouse, if I right-click on the image, I can choose Save Picture As, and then I save it on my floppy disk (the A: drive) like I would any file. I can keep the file name it already has ("tiedbks") or give it a new one; I'll keep the same one. And it prompts me that it is going to save it as a .gif file, which is fine. (The other option you can choose for your graphics is .jpg.) I then click Save, and that's it. Easy!

Now, I just want to check and make sure it worked.

> [Continue to demonstrate.]

In my browser, I am going to choose File, then Open, then Browse to find my A drive. Once there, I'll choose All Files in the Files of Type box, and there I see the "tiedbks.gif" file. If I select that, choose Open, and then choose OK, it brings the image up in my browser. And there it is.

As I said, choose any graphic you like; it can be library-related or not. We'll be working with it in the next session. I only ask that it not be too big a file. Less than 10K would be best.

You can also, if you wish, bring in an image of your own—for example, if you have digitized photographs, or have access to a scanner or a graphics program. Again, though, please don't make the image file too big. And if you do bring in your own image, please also spend some time looking at these clip art sites.

Are there any questions about this assignment?

COPY TO HARD DRIVE/REMINDER TO BRING BACK FLOPPY DISK

Before we end, like last time, I want you to copy your updated HTML document to your hard drive.

[Do this yourself as well, so that everyone can follow along with you.]

Click on the Windows Start button in the lower left corner, choose Programs, then choose Internet Explorer. Select the Floppy (A) drive. Select your HTML document (mine is "Bill's Home Page.html") and then drag it over to the C: drive and release, so that it will copy it to the hard drive. And go ahead and replace the older file on your hard drive.

[If they saved to a subdirectory on the hard drive the last time, have them choose that same one again, so that the older file is replaced.]

Once you have copied the file, exit out of Internet Explorer by clicking on the X in the upper right corner, or by choosing File/Close.

Again, though, please remember to bring your floppies back with you, which will include both your HTML file and your image.

REVIEW

Again, we have covered a lot today. We reinforced how to create the three kinds of lists: unordered, ordered, and definition. And mostly we focused on creating links. We learned how to use the <A> anchor tag and the HREF parameter to create links to external documents and files, both absolute links and relative links. We also learned how to create internal links for long documents. And we learned how to create an e-mail link, as well. Finally, we went over some troubleshooting tips, and ways to make your documents easier to scan for the trouble spots.

See you next time!

10
Introduction to HTML (Part 3): Graphics and Color

Handouts for this workshop follow page 197.

OVERVIEW

Who

This third HTML training workshop in the series is designed for trainees who have already taken "Introduction to HTML (Part 1): Structure and Text" and "Introduction to HTML (Part 2): Links and Troubleshooting." Preferably the same group of people will go through this training series together, but it is not necessary.

What

This is a series of three hands-on workshops providing a basic introduction to HTML. Part 3 introduces graphics (creation, inclusion, alignment with text, and hyperlinking), and delves into color (background and font). It also points to future directions (other HTML and Web development features, future classes, and internal organizational procedures).

Where

Like the first two sessions, this training workshop is designed for a computer lab with space for ten students and an instructor (11 PCs total). The instructor's PC has projection. Each of the computers has Internet access, Microsoft Internet Explorer (or another graphical browser), Windows 95 or Windows 98 (this workshop can be adapted easily to another operating system), and Notepad (or another plain text editor).

When

It should take place soon after Part 2, but allowing enough time for everyone to complete the assignment. One week is ideal. This session lasts one hour.

Why

The objectives of this three-part series are for the trainees to be able to (1) explain the concepts of HTML; (2) create basic Web pages using correct HTML (text, links, and graphics); and (3) use appropriate resources effectively for further learning and reference.

The objectives for Part 3 are for the trainees to be able to (1) include graphics effectively in their Web pages; (2) use background and font colors effectively in their Web pages; and (3) explain how what they have learned in this introductory series fits into the larger picture of Web development and of Web site creation at the library.

WORKSHOP AGENDA

Again, this agenda moves quickly into hands-on work and an assistant would be helpful, but not necessary.

Also, once again, there are a hundred things you could cover in this session, but could never get through in the time allotted. Focus on "need-to-know" information.

WELCOME BACK

- Assignments Review (0:00–0:05)
- Objectives for This Session (0:05–0:08)

IMAGES

- Creation (0:08–0:13)
- Inline Images (0:13–0:18)
- Alignment (0:18–0:23)
- Alternate Text (0:23–0:28)
- Hyperlinks (0:28–0:33)

COLOR

- Background (0:33–0:38)
- Text and Links (0:38–0:43)
- RGB (0:43–0:48)

OTHER HTML AND WEB DEVELOPMENT FEATURES (0:48–0:54)

INTERNAL EDITORIAL/WEB PRODUCTION PROCEDURES (0:54–0:58)

REVIEW (0:58–1:00)

SAMPLE SCRIPT

Again, this session assumes that you are using Internet Explorer, Windows 95 or Windows 98, and Notepad. It will be easy to make the necessary adjustments if you have a different browser, operating system, or text editor.

Graphics and color are complicated topics. You will have to work on a balancing act: making the session simple and fun, motivating the trainees by showing them how much they can do, but also conveying how rich and complicated these issues really are.

Welcome Back

ASSIGNMENTS REVIEW (0:00–0:05)

Welcome back! How did everyone do with the linking assignment, to create links from the three Web sites you listed in your definition list? Did everyone do OK with that?

[*Get responses.*]

Let me just quickly show you mine.

[*Bring up your HTML document on the projector.*]

<DL>
<DT><A HREF="http://lcweb.loc.gov/">The Library of Congress</A>
<DD>The Library of Congress has some terrific exhibits up on the Web, plus their catalog is searchable.
<DT><A HREF="http://www.imdb.com/">The Internet Movie Database</A>
<DD>This site is great for movie trivia; it lists credits for just about every movie you could think of, is fully searchable, and offers links to other resources.
<DT><A HREF="http://www.akc.org/">The American Kennel Club</A>
<DD>This organization provides extensive information about many different kinds of dog breeds; the pictures are great, too.
</DL>

Notice that I kept the structural tag (<DT>) outside of the anchor (<A>) tags. Does everyone have something that looks like this?

OK, and how about the image assignment? Would one of you like to show us the image you brought?

[Have a volunteer come up with his or her floppy; display the image on the projector. Ask where he or she found—or created—it. If you have time, have another volunteer come up.]

Was everyone else able to get an image, either from one of the clip art resources on the handout, or from some other place?

[If anyone is without an image, take two minutes to walk them through the process of capturing an image from one of the clip art resources. Do this quickly.]

OBJECTIVES FOR THIS SESSION (0:05–0:08)

In Part 1 we focused on the basics for structure and text in HTML. In Part 2 we concentrated on links (really the heart of HTML), and also on troubleshooting. Today we are going to turn to graphics and color. We have three objectives for this session.

[Have the three objectives written on a board or flip chart.]

By the end of the session today, we will be able to (1) include graphics effectively in our Web pages; (2) use background and font colors effectively in our Web pages; and (3) explain how what we have learned in this introductory series fits into the larger picture of Web development and of Web site creation at the library.
Let's begin!

Images

CREATION (0:08–0:13)

OK, we are talking about graphics and images. Where do you get these graphics?

[Get responses and write on flip chart or board. Supply any responses that you don't receive.]

Some of the places to find or create graphics and images are:

- *Free clip art resources* on the Web, like the ones we already looked at on the handout. These often contain a variety of great graphics and icons—buttons, bars, pictures, and so on.
- *Commercial clip art and stock photography services*, such as Corbis

(*http://www.corbis.com/*). Also, many commercial Web page creation software packages, such as Microsoft's FrontPage and Adobe's PageMill, include thousands of images and graphics that you can use.

- *Commercial graphics programs*, from simple programs like Paint to more expensive graphics packages like Adobe Photoshop and ClarisDraw, allow you to create and edit graphics.
- *Digital cameras* allow you to take digitized photographs that you can use on your Web page. While still expensive, good ones are starting to come down in price.
- *Scanners* allow you to scan anything—photographs, pictures, your hand—and turn it into a digitized image. Again, the price of scanners has come down significantly over the last couple of years.

Lots of these tools work together. For example, you can work with a graphics editing program to touch up images that you have scanned.

I want to emphasize a couple of points here. One is that, while they can be fun and can create great effects, some graphics programs are fairly complicated and sophisticated; they take a big time commitment to learn. The other point, though, is that you can do a lot with very little; for instance, the free clip art sites are great resources.

But be careful about "stealing" images off the Web. You must make sure you have permission, or that the images are in the public domain. While it is technically easy to copy any image you want off the Web, remember that copyright laws apply, and you can't just take something that you don't have rights to.

Also, remember that graphics and images are typically larger files than text files, and they therefore take more time to load—which can frustrate the reader of your page. Use them judiciously, and only include them when they really enhance the page and are worth the extra time it will take. And try not to use image files that are very, very big.

INLINE IMAGES (0:13–0:18)

OK, let's include our images in our Web pages. Please open Notepad and your HTML document on your diskette.

[Everyone opens HTML documents in Notepad.]

Does everyone have that open? Now, the main tag for images in HTML is the <IMG> image tag, along with the SRC parameter (which stands for source). I am going to add this to the end of my HTML document, right after my last bit of text, but before the final closing FONT and BODY tags. Everyone do this along with me.

[Demonstrate.]

This is what I type: <IMG SRC=

The source is the name and location of the image file; in that way, it is similar to the reference in a hypertext link. This could be an external URL for an image, or it could be a local file. We are going to use our local image file on our floppies, so we only need to create a relative link—just the name of the file itself, since it is in the same directory as our HTML document. My image file is called "tiedbks.gif," so this is what I end up with:

[Continue to demonstrate.]

<IMG SRC="tiedbks.gif">

Everyone should put the name of their image file in the quotation marks, and don't forget the closing angle bracket. If you can't remember the name of your image file, in Notepad you can choose File, then Open, and take a look on your A: drive. Also, don't forget the three letter extension—probably either .gif or .jpg. These are the most common image formats for the Web, although some others work, as well.

Does everyone have something similar to what I have?

Let's take a look in our browsers and see if it worked. Don't forget to save your changes in Notepad. Then launch your browser if it isn't open already, and open your HTML document in your browser. Scroll down to the bottom of the page to see if your image came up. Did that work for everyone?

[Spend a minute or two helping anyone who is having problems.]

That's the basic way to add images to your Web page. These images are sometimes called "inline images" because they are pasted onto the page along with the text. As I said, the two most common image formats for Web pages are .gif and .jpg. One of the sites listed on your handout—Preparing Graphics for the Web (*http://www.servtech.com/public/dougg/graphics/*)—has a lot of really useful information on using GIF and JPEG image file formats.

ALIGNMENT (0:18–0:23)

We just put our image on the left side of the page below all the text. But there are other layouts that we can use on our image and our text. Let's look at those now.

First, let's create some text. In your HTML document, below your image, write a little something about your image and where you got it. For instance, I am going to write:

[Demonstrate.]

I got the image of these books from a site called "Library Graphics." This site has many images related to libraries, such as books and computers.

Again, it doesn't really matter what you write; we just need a sentence or two of text to work with. Everyone please do that now.

[Everyone writes their text.]

Let's save our changes, and take a look in our browsers. Notice how, when we don't put any <P> paragraph tags around the text or the image, the default is to align the bottom of the image with the text that follows. That looks pretty good. It's also possible, though, to use the ALIGN attribute to do different things. We haven't looked at the ALIGN attribute before, but it can be really useful in a number of ways.

Let's align the text with the image a little differently. Let's insert ALIGN=TOP into our <IMG> image tag, so that I end up with:

[Demonstrate.]

<IMG ALIGN=TOP SRC="tiedbks.gif">

Everyone please insert ALIGN=TOP into your image tag, save the changes, and take a look in your browser.

Notice that this aligns only one line of text next to the top of the image, and then jumps to below the image for the rest of the text. That looks a little funny with this image and this amount of text, but it could look good sometimes—for example, if you only had one line of text.

Similarly, let's change the coding to align the text to the center of the image. That looks like this:

[Demonstrate.]

<IMG ALIGN=CENTER SRC="tiedbks.gif">

Everyone do that, save the changes, and take a look.

As you see, this does the same as the top alignment, affecting only the first line of text, except now the first line is in the center of the image. Again, it looks a little funny in this case.

One way to get around this problem is to align the image to the left or the right. The default is the left, but if you specify the alignment, it will put the entire text (or as much as fits) next to the image on the right, starting at the top. Similarly, if you align the image on the right of the page, the browser will put the text along the left, starting at the top. Let's do that now. I am going to change my coding to:

[Demonstrate.]

    <IMG ALIGN=RIGHT SRC="tiedbks.gif">

Everyone, please try that, save the changes, and take a look.
That looks pretty good, I think.
Now I want to show you one more thing about alignment. You can also align text or images to the center or right on a Web page using the ALIGN attribute in the <P> paragraph tag. This will work for any text or any image enclosed with the paragraph tags. Let's try that now.
First, let's get rid of our ALIGN=RIGHT attribute in the <IMG> image tag.

[Demonstrate.]

Next, let's enclose our image in paragraph tags, and also the following text in separate paragraph tags. So this is what I end up with:

    <P><IMG SRC="tiedbks.gif"></P>
    <P>I got the image of these books from a site called "Library Graphics." This site has many images related to libraries, such as books and computers.</P>

If I want to align the image or the text to the right or to the center, I just add ALIGN=RIGHT or ALIGN=CENTER to the initial paragraph tag. For instance:

[Demonstrate.]

    <P ALIGN=CENTER><IMG SRC="tiedbks.gif"></P>
    <P ALIGN=CENTER>I got the image of these books from a site called "Library Graphics." This site has many images related to libraries, such as books and computers.</P>

This aligns both the image and the text in the center of the page.
Everyone, please try that.

[Walk around and help anyone who is stuck or has questions.]

Everyone got that? Remember, we could do the same to the right. And also remember, you can use this ALIGN attribute with any paragraph tag, for any text or image.

We have tried a lot of different alignments of image and text, and there are a lot of different options and combinations. The best thing is to play around with different alignments until something looks right to you.

Are there any questions at this point?

ALTERNATE TEXT (0:23–0:28)

One thing we should always remember when we are creating Web pages is that not everyone uses a browser that displays images. Text-only browsers for the World Wide Web are available; you may have heard of the browser Lynx, for example. In addition, some people turn off the image display in their browsers as they surf around; this is especially true for people who may not have the fastest connections in the world (people using the Web from home, for instance) and who don't want to be slowed down by a lot of images, which take a long time to load.

Therefore, it is good HTML practice to include, along with your images, some alternate text that will be displayed in non-graphical browsers and browsers that have their image display temporarily turned off. This text tells users what they are missing; in the case of people who have temporarily turned their images off, they can then decide whether or not to display this image. Including alternate text is easy to do and increases accessibility for all users.

You insert alternate text with the ALT attribute of the <IMG> image tag. It looks like this:

[Demonstrate.]

<P ALIGN=CENTER><IMG SRC="tiedbks.gif" ALT="Books Tied Together"></P>

Now I am going to save my changes, and go to my browser. I want to turn off my images temporarily, so that I can see whether it worked. I do this under View/Internet Options/Advanced; then I uncheck the Show Pictures box and click OK. Now I hit Refresh. We see the icon for the image that is not displayed, and the alternate text is there.

Now, everyone please insert alternate text for your image, and check it in your browser.

[Return to your HTML document in Notepad and display it on the projector, so that people can refer to it. Walk around and help anyone who is stuck or has questions.]

Did that work for everybody? Does anybody have any questions?

You should always, always include alternate text for your images. Now, before we go on, let's change our options in our browsers back to display images again.

[Demonstrate.]

Remember, that's View/Internet Options/Advanced; then check the Show Pictures box and click OK. Hit Refresh and the image should display again.

HYPERLINKS (0:28–0:33)

Another thing you can do with an image is to make it hyperlinked, so that someone can click on it and be taken to another file or document. We have all seen buttons, dots, arrows, and larger pictures and graphics that hyperlink to other files. Let's make our image hyperlinked now.

We do this the same way we make text a hyperlink—with the <A> anchor tag and the HREF attribute. So I am going to surround my image tagging with the link tagging. I am going to have the link go to the library. (Since the image is of books, that makes some sense.) Here is what it looks like:

[Demonstrate.]

```
<P ALIGN=CENTER><A HREF="http://www.spl.lib.wa.us/"><IMG
SRC="tiedbks.gif" ALT="Books Tied Together"></A></P>
```

Notice that I have surrounded the <IMG> image tagging with the link tagging, and the link is to the URL for the Seattle Public Library. It looks just like any other hypertext link we have created, except now it is surrounding an image rather than some text. Let's take a look. I am going to save my changes and refresh my browser.

[Continue to demonstrate.]

And here it is in the browser. Notice that the image is now surrounded by a border, which indicates that the image is hot. Plus, when I put my mouse arrow over the image, it now turns into a hand, again indicating that you can click on the image. And when I click, it takes me to the Seattle Public Library.

Now I want everyone please to make your image a hyperlink, and you can link it anywhere you want, to any URL. Usually, of course, you'll want your image and the destination location to make sense—for instance, an arrow forward going to the next logical document in a series, or a photograph of a library going to more information about that library.

Please insert the hyperlink tagging in your image now.

[Return to your HTML document in Notepad, so that people can refer to it. Walk around and help anyone who is stuck or has questions.]

Did that work out for everybody?

Now, let's play with the border size a little bit. You can set border size with the BORDER attribute of the <IMG> image tag. You would type *BORDER=* and then some number, which is the border width in pixels. So, for example . . .

[Demonstrate.]

. . . I am going to set the BORDER for my image at 8, like this:

<P ALIGN=CENTER><A HREF="http://www.spl.lib.wa.us/"><IMG SRC="tiedbks.gif" BORDER=8 ALT="Books Tied Together"></A></P>

And this is what it looks like:

[Display in browser.]

It made the border noticeably thicker. I can also make the border smaller than normal, for example, if I set it to size 1. And I can even make it disappear altogether, if I set the border to equal zero, like this:

[Demonstrate in Notepad, and display in browser.]

<P ALIGN=CENTER><A HREF="http://www.spl.lib.wa.us/"><IMG SRC="tiedbks.gif" BORDER=0 ALT="Books Tied Together"></A></P>

I like the looks of that, but there is a danger that when you have no border people will not easily recognize that the image is a link.

Why doesn't everyone play around a little bit with border size, and set it to what you think looks good, even to no border, if you wish.

[Return to your HTML document in Notepad, so that people can refer to it. Walk around and help anyone who is stuck or has questions.]

Are there any questions about borders? Any questions about images and graphics, before we turn to text and background color?

Color

BACKGROUND (0:33–0:38)

Now let's return to color. We touched briefly on color in our first session, when we made some of our text green. Let's take a little closer look at color now.

By default, most browsers display the text of Web pages in black and the background in gray or white. In addition, as you probably know, people can change those browser defaults on the user end. But, as a Web page creator, you can also override those defaults and add both background and text color to your Web pages.

Before we really get started, though, let me just say a quick word about design and color. There is a reason that the default is black text on a white or gray background; that's because dark text on a light background is the easiest for most people to read. Anything else—light on dark, dark on darker, and so forth—can be problematic, especially for people with visual impairments. We have all seen pages where the colors make it nearly impossible to read. Printing can be another problem area, especially if you are using light text on a dark background; usually, the printer will print the background as white, and this will make the light text difficult or impossible to read. So think carefully about using color and whether it is really necessary. And preview your choices, on a number of different computer monitors, if possible.

OK, with those caveats and warnings, let's begin! The color attributes for both background and text go within the BODY tag. Let's start with the background. Everyone watch me for a minute.

[Demonstrate.]

I am going to go up to my initial BODY tag and add the background color attribute BGCOLOR= . After the equal sign I can put in a number, which stands for the RGB (red, green, blue) value of the color I've chosen; we'll return to RGB numbers in a minute. I can also put in one of 16 named colors, which correspond to the basic VGA set on most PCs. These colors are . . .

[Have these written on a board or flip chart.]

. . . Aqua, Black, Blue, Fuchsia, Gray, Green, Lime, Maroon, Navy, Olive, Purple, Red, Silver, Teal, White, and Yellow. Most browsers also accept other colors, but this is the standard set.

I'll try the first one: Aqua. So my tagging will look like:

<BODY BGCOLOR="Aqua">

I am going to save my changes and take a look in my browser.

[Continue to demonstrate.]

That's pretty—well, sort of!

Now, I want everyone to work on their own documents and try out some of these background colors. Check out a few in your browser; see if you hit on any that you like.

[Walk around and help anyone who is stuck or has questions.]

How did that work out for anyone? Anyone find colors that you liked? Any that you *didn't* like?

By the way, it's also possible to insert images as backgrounds, often in combination with background color. I'm sure you've all seen horrible background images on some Web pages! Clouds or a brick wall or some other image that makes the text impossible to read. Well, background images can also sometimes be used to nice effect. But I'm going to let you learn how to do that on your own! (Hint: it also goes in the BODY tag.)

TEXT AND LINKS (0:38–0:43)

Now, we can do the same thing with text color. Like the background color attribute that we just learned about, the TEXT attribute also goes in the BODY tag. The same colors work. Here's what the tagging looks like:

<BODY BGCOLOR="White" TEXT="Navy">

By the way, I changed my background color to white, since that's my favorite background color. Remember, simpler is better! And lighter backgrounds are usually better, too. For contrast I decided I want my text to be navy. I'll save, and let's take a look.

[Continue to demonstrate.]

So, you see, the background is now white and the text is navy blue. Notice, too, that the text I put in green in the first session—the word "large"—is still green. That's because I used the <FONT COLOR=GREEN> tagging for that word, and that overrides the base text color you set with the TEXT attribute in the BODY tag. So use the TEXT attribute in the BODY tag to set a base text color throughout the document, and then you can set different colors for particular words or sections of a document using the COLOR attribute in the FONT tag. Does that make sense?

Now, I want everyone to work on your own documents again, and try out some text colors, in combination with some background colors.

[Walk around and help anyone who is stuck or has questions. After a few minutes, go on to the following.]

Now I want everyone to pause for a minute and look up here. In addition to setting the color of the regular text to something other than the default, you can also set the color of the hyperlinks in your Web page to colors other than the defaults. Here are those attributes:

[Write these four attributes on a board or flip chart.]

- We already know that TEXT is for regular text.
- LINK is for unvisited links (links the user hasn't clicked on yet). The default for these in most browsers is blue.
- VLINK is for visited links. The default for these in many browsers is purple.
- ALINK is for active links—in other words, the color that the link turns to when you click on it, but before you release the mouse button. In many browsers the default for this is red.

You can set all of these to be the same color, or all different, or some the same and some different. You just add these attributes to the BODY tag, like you did with the background color and TEXT attributes. If you leave any of them out, that's fine; the browser will just display its default colors.

I am going to set some link colors in my document.

[Demonstrate.]

And this is what I end up with:

```
<BODY BGCOLOR="White" TEXT="Navy" LINK="Red" VLINK=
"Maroon" ALINK="Yellow">
```

And I'll save that and take a look in my browser.

[Continue to demonstrate.]

Now my background is white, my text is navy, the links are red, the links I have already clicked on are maroon, and notice that when I click on a link (before I let go of the mouse button) it turns yellow.

So everyone, please continue to work with your background and text colors in your documents for a couple of minutes, and maybe now add some link colors, too.

[Walk around and help anyone who is stuck or has questions.]

How did that work for everyone?

RGB (RED, GREEN, BLUE) (0:43–0:48)

We have been using named colors, but as we see, that has restricted us to a pretty limited color palette. The other way to specify background, text, and link colors is to use what is known as their RGB values; RGB stands for red, green, blue. These are six-character, hexadecimal numbers—really, a sequence of letters and numbers—which correspond to individual colors. These six characters are actually three two-characters sequences; each two-character sequence represents how much red, green, and blue is in the color, from 00 (none) to FF (fully saturated). For instance, 000000 is all black (no color), FF0000 is red, 0000FF is blue, and FFFFFF is all white (total saturation with all three colors). Various combinations create other colors and brightness in between.

I know this can be confusing. That's the bad news. The good news is that using RGB values opens up the available color palette. The other good news is that there are resources to help you find the hexadecimal value for the color you want. Many commercial HTML editors, Web page creation applications, and graphics programs include tools that allow you to map colors to their hexadecimal values. In addition, there are free services on the Web that do this for you, and I want to show you one of these now. It's called the ColorCenter (*http://www.hidaho.com/colorcenter/*), and it's included on your handout.

[Go to the site and demonstrate.]

You see that the ColorCenter has a drop-down menu that allows you to select background, text, link, visited link, and active link. I'll choose one— background—and then I can select a color from the palette at the bottom. As I do this, you see that it actually changes the color of the background of this page. Notice, too, that it has a BODY tag here on the page, and it changed the hexadecimal color value of the background color attribute for that tag. That value matches the background color I just chose. I can easily try different colors, and it automatically updates the value for me. I can even change the brightness. And I can do the same thing for the text and the various types of links.

[Continue to demonstrate for a minute.]

Then, when I have it how I want it to look, I can just copy and paste the whole BODY string into my own page.

Neat, huh? Are there any questions?

Now, everyone please go to the ColorCenter site and play around with it a little bit. If you want, you can then paste your new colors with their hexadecimal values into your own page.

[Walk around and help anyone who is stuck or has questions.]

Other HTML and Web Development Features (0:48–0:54)

We have covered an amazing amount of ground over the last three sessions, and you now have the knowledge and ability to create fine Web pages. You also, I hope, know how to turn to other resources for help and further learning; the resources listed on your handout are excellent places to start.

We have, though, only scratched the surface of HTML and Web development, and I want to give you a little taste of what else is going on and what else there is to learn.

[Tie the following to any further workshops in the training series, if appropriate. Write the major features mentioned on a board or flip chart.]

In terms of HTML presentation and design, creating *tables* and *frames* opens up a lot of new possibilities, and these are easily within the capabilities of everyone here.

A more recent and exciting developing in Web design is what is known as *Cascading Style Sheets*. Cascading Style Sheets (CSS) allow you to create a separate document and attach it to your HTML documents, and this style sheet tells the browser how to format the documents—for example, fonts, colors, margins. Multiple HTML documents can be linked to one style sheet, so you can change one style sheet and thereby change the look of an entire set of Web pages. Style sheets "cascade" hierarchically—different style sheets can be used for different sections of a site, and a subsequent sheet can override the settings of sheets before it. In this separation of style and structure, a lot more control is given over to the Web developer, and it's a very exciting development. Again, Cascading Style Sheets are well within the capabilities of everyone here to learn, and a number of resources on your handout can help, including Next Generation HTML: The Big Picture (*http://wdvl.com/Authoring/Languages/XML/Overview/*) and the Web site for the World Wide Web Consortium, known as W3C (*http://www.w3.org/MarkUp/MarkUp.html*).

Some more advanced technologies, some of them fairly new, require a bit more programming skill. You may have heard of *Dynamic HTML* (or DHTML), which are HTML extensions that allow for dynamic content in Web pages based on user input and other factors.

Much of the Web is driven by database technology, often with *Common Gateway Interface* (CGI) scripts or programs that act as the go-between for a Web-based form and a database of information. CGI scripts are typically written in programming languages such as C++, Perl, Java, and Visual Basic. Computer programmers are really the only folks who have the training to write these back-end types of programs. However, *Web-based forms* (the interface that the user sees) are well within the capabilities of anyone here to learn quickly.

XML stands for eXtensible Markup Language. It is a version of SGML (Standard Generalized Markup Language) designed specifically for Web documents that enables designers to create their own customized tags. XML is still in its beginning stages, but it is something to watch. If you want to learn more, you might turn to Next Generation HTML: The Big Picture (*http://wdvl.com/Authoring/Languages/XML/Overview/*).

We didn't really touch on *multimedia*, such as audio and video, but certainly this is an exciting area for Web development. While, again, mastering these skills requires semester-long courses, being able to include simple audio and video files with your Web pages is absolutely something anyone can learn. Many of the resources on the handout can help you, including BUILDER.COM (*http://builder.com/*) and WebReference.com (*http://www.webreference.com/*).

And finally, we talked a little about this throughout our three sessions, but I really encourage you to think and learn more about *design* issues for the Web. While we may not become graphic designers, some tried and true design rules can help us create better Web pages. I encourage you to take a look at: Web Design for Librarians (*http://scc01.rutgers.edu/SCCHome/web.htm*), Website Design Guidelines for Public Libraries (*http://web0.tiac.net/users/mpl/guidelines.html*), and the Yale C/AIM Web Style Guide (*http://info.med.yale.edu/caim/manual/index.html*).

Internal Editorial/Web Production Procedures (0:54–0:58)

[At this point, if appropriate, spend some time discussing internal procedures within the library for developing and updating the library's Web site—people,

editorial processes, etc. This may have to be a fairly general discussion. You also won't have time to train everyone on procedures for uploading to the server. (This might be a useful module for a future training session.)]

Review (0:58–1:00)

Before we break, I just want to review quickly what we went over today. First, we reinforced how to create links, by linking to the three sites we listed in our definition list.

Next, we turned to images and graphics. We learned how to find lots of available graphics through free clip art resources on the Web, and we also learned that we can create graphics with a number of programs and tools. We learned how to include an image in our Web page with the <IMG> image tag, and how to align the image and the text in different ways. We learned that it is important to include alternate text using the ALT attribute, and we also learned how to make an image a hyperlink.

Finally, we went over different ways to create color for your background and for your text, using both hexadecimal values and named colors.

That's it! Please don't forget to save your changes and take your floppy disk and handouts with you. And keep learning and creating!

INTRODUCTION TO HTML (PART 1) AGENDA

Introduction

- Welcome
- Prerequisites
- Objectives for this Session

What Is HTML?

- Definition
- View Source
- Tags

Tools

- Text Editors
- HTML Editors/Web Authoring Tools
- Word Processors

Basic Structural Tags

- <HTML>
- <HEAD>
- <TITLE>
- <BODY>
- Save and View

Other Structural and Presentation Tags

- Heading
- Paragraph
- Line Break
- Horizontal Rule

Text Formatting

- Bold
- Italics
- Font: Size, Color, Face
- Logical Tags

Assignment: Lists

- Lists: Unordered, Ordered, Definition

Review and Wrap Up

- Copy Document to Hard Drive/Reminder to Bring Back Floppy
- Review

INTRODUCTION TO HTML (PART 2) AGENDA

Assignment Review: Lists

- Demonstration of Lists
- Objectives for this Session

Absolute Links

- Hotlinks
- Providing exact path

Relative Links

- Link to another document in same directory
- Link to another document in same subdirectory

Internal Links

- Link to another part in same document
- Advantages of internal links

Mail Links

- Mailto reference

Troubleshooting

- All upper- or lowercase
- Each command on new line
- Files saved and checked regularly
- Things to watch for

Assignments

- Assignment #1: Links
- Assignment #2: Images
- Copy to Hard Drive/Reminder to Bring Back Disk

Review

INTRODUCTION TO HTML (PART 3) AGENDA

Welcome Back

- Assignment Review
- Objectives for this Session

Images

- Creation
- Inline Images
- Alignment
- Alternate Text
- Hyperlinks

Color

- Background
- Text and Links
- RGB

Other HTML and Web Development Features

Internal Editorial/Web Production Procedures

Review

HTML TAGS COVERED

Structural and Presentation Tags

HTML: \<HTML> \</HTML>
Head: \<HEAD> \</HEAD>
Title: \<TITLE> \</TITLE>
Body: \<BODY> \</BODY>
Heading: \<H#> \</H#>
Paragraph: \<P> \</P>
Line Break: \
Horizontal Rule: \<HR>

Text Formatting

Bold: \<B> \</B>
Italics: \<I> \</I>
Font Size: \<FONT SIZE=#> \</FONT>
Font Color: \<FONT COLOR=XXX> \</FONT>
Font Typeface: \<FONT FACE=XXX> \</FONT>
Emphasis: \<EM> \</EM>
Strong Emphasis: \<STRONG> \</STRONG>
Citation: \<CITE> \</CITE>
Unordered List: \<UL> \<LI>…\</UL>
Ordered List: \<OL> \<LI>…\</OL>
Definition List: \<DL> \<DT> \<DD>…\</DL>

Links and Anchors

External Link: \<A HREF="URL/File"> \</A>
Internal Link: \<A HREF="#Named Anchor"> \</A>
Named Anchor: \<A Name="Named Anchor"> \</A>
Mail Link: \<A HREF="mailto:email address"> \</A>

Images and Color

Image: \<IMG SRC="*File Name*">
\<IMG> tag attributes:
    Alignment: ALIGN=TOP/CENTER/BOTTOM
    Alternate Text: ALT="*text*"
\<BODY> attributes:
    Background Color: BGCOLOR=[*Named Color or RGB Value*]
    Text Color: TEXT=[*Named Color or RGB Value*]
    Link Color: LINK=[*Named Color or RGB Value*]

Visited Link: VLINK=[*Named Color or RGB Value*]
Active Link: ALINK=[*Named Color or RGB Value*]

FURTHER READING AND RESOURCES

Books

Castro, Elizabeth. *HTML 4 for the World Wide Web: Visual QuickStart Guide.* 3rd ed. Berkeley, Calif.: Peachpit Press, 1997.
    Provides clear references to HTML tags, including new HTML 4 tags.
Graham, Ian S. *HTML 4.0 Sourcebook.* 4th ed. New York: John Wiley, 1998.
    A basic reference on all HTML. Includes newer features such as Cascading Style Sheets and Dynamic HTML.
Ibanez, Ardith, and Natalie Zee. *HTML Artistry: More than Code.* Indianapolis, Ind.: Hayden Books, 1998.
    Focuses on practical Web page design issues. Includes many examples.
Junion-Metz, Gail, and Brad Stephens. *Creating a Power Website: HTML 3, Tables, Imagemaps, Frames, and Forms.* New York: Neal-Schuman Publishers, 1998.
    Covers advanced HTML features using library examples and practical exercises.
Lemay, Laura, and Arman Danesh. *Teach Yourself Web Publishing with HTML 4 in a Week.* 4th ed. Indianapolis, Ind.: Sams, 1997.
    Includes daily tutorials, from the basics through to Dynamic HTML.
Tittel, Ed, et al. *HTML 4 For Dummies.* Foster City, Calif.: IDG Books Worldwide, 1998.
    An introduction to HTML, from the basics to newer features. Look for other HTML and Web Publishing books in the "For Dummies" series.

Periodicals

Internet World.
    Offers industry news and feature articles for Internet professionals. Online version available at *http://www.iw.com/*.
PC World.
    Provides coverage of Internet issues and products, as well as PC product reviews. Online version available at *http://www.pcworld.com/*
Wired.
    Offers feature articles and commentary on technology and online culture. Online version available at *http://www.wired.com/wired/* See also Hotwired (*http://www.hotwired.com/*).

Web Sites

The Bare Bones Guide to HTML

http://werbach.com/barebones/

A basic listing of HTML tags. Useful as a quick reference.

Barry's Clip Art Server

http://www.barrysclipart.com/

A large collection of clip art, plus links to other clip art resources.

Bobby

http://www.cast.org/bobby/

A free program that analyzes Web pages for their accessibility to people with disabilities, and their compatibility with various browsers.

BUILDER.COM

http://builder.com/

Includes articles, tools, and resources for Web site developers. From CNET (The Computer Network).

Clip Art Review

http://www.webplaces.com/html/clipart.htm

An extensive collection of free graphics and images on the Web, arranged by category. Also provides a link to Clip Art Searcher (a service that simultaneously searches a number of search engines for clip art) and links to other clip art collections.

ColorCenter

http://www.hidaho.com/colorcenter/

Includes information and resources for working with color in your Web pages, including a color chart with corresponding hexadecimal values.

Cool Graphics

http://www.fishnet.net/~gini/cool/

Annotated directory of free and low-cost graphic sites on the Web.

The HMTL Writers Guild

http://www.hwg.org/

Offers resources for Web designers and information about the organization.

Introduction to HTML

http://www.cwru.edu/help/introHTML/toc.html

An excellent online tutorial for beginners.

Library Clipart Collection

http://www.netins.net/showcase/meyers/library_clipart/clipart.html

A large collection of book-related clip art, available for downloading and use.

Library Graphics

http://www.geocities.com/Athens/Acropolis/2161/clipart/index.htm

Another large collection of public-domain images, both book and computer-related. Includes links to other similar resources.

NCSA (at UIUC) Beginner's Guide to HTML
http://www.ncsa.uiuc.edu/General/Internet/WWW/HTMLPrimer.html
A classic guide, updated for the most current HTML specification.

(The New) Mag's List of HTML Editors
http://www.hypernews.org/HyperNews/get/www/html/editors.html
An extensive directory of commercial and noncommercial HTML editors.

Next Generation HTML: The Big Picture
http://wdvl.com/Authoring/Languages/XML/Overview/
Examines advanced and future-oriented features, such as XML, Cascading Style Sheets, Dynamic HTML, and the Document Object Model (DOM).

Preparing Graphics for the Web
http://www.servtech.com/public/dougg/graphics/
Provides practical information on using GIF and JPEG image file formats.

Rob Schluter's HTML Tag List
http://utopia.knoware.nl/users/schluter/doc/tags/
Another HTML tag list, with examples, tips, and tricks.

W3C's HTML Home Page
http://www.w3.org/MarkUp/MarkUp.html
From the World Wide Web Consortium (W3C). Provides the latest official HTML specifications (including HTML 4.0), a guide for HTML beginners, accessibility guidelines, information on XML and Cascading Style Sheets, an HTML validation service, and other resources.

Web Design for Librarians
http://scc01.rutgers.edu/SCCHome/web.htm
Offers practical Web design techniques and advice. From the Scholarly Communication Center at Rutgers University.

Web Design Group
http://www.htmlhelp.com/
A general resource for Web site developers with an HTML tagging reference guide, design advice, tools information, and other resources.

Web Site Garage
http://www.websitegarage.com/
Checks links, browser compatibility, spelling, and HTML code. Also performs other Web site maintenance functions.

WebReference.com
http://www.webreference.com/
Includes news, online tutorials, and articles for Webmasters.

Website Design Guidelines for Public Libraries
http://web0.tiac.net/users/mpl/guidelines.html
Provides basic suggestions for the content and design of library Web sites. From the Milton Public Library.

WebTechs Validation Service

http://valsvc.webtechs.com/

An easy-to-use, free HTML validation service.

Writing for the Web: A Primer for Librarians

http://bones.med.ohio-state.edu/eric/papers/primer/webdocs.html

An introduction to general concepts and technologies for Web site creation. Offers many links to further information on particular topics.

Yahoo! HTML Editors

http://www.yahoo.com/Computers_and_Internet/Software/Internet/World_Wide_Web/ HTML_Editors/

Yahoo's directory of HTML editors, both commercial and shareware.

Yale C/AIM Web Style Guide

http://info.med.yale.edu/caim/manual/index.html

Offers advice and techniques related to style and design issues.

Index

ABOUT THE AUTHOR

William Hollands received a B.A. in English from Williams College, an M.A. in literature from Cambridge University, and an M.I.L.S. from the University of Michigan's School of Information and Library Studies (now the School of Information). While at Michigan, he became interested in the Internet, library instruction, and user education.

His first professional library position was with the New York Public Library's Science, Industry, and Business Library, where he was in charge of a widespread technology training program for the staff.

In 1995, he became the New York Public Library's first Internet Librarian (later Web Coordinator) for the system's 85 branch libraries. In this position, in addition to being responsible for development of the libraries' Web pages, he coordinated an extensive, ongoing Internet training program which trained over 1,000 staff members on the basics of the Web, using search engines effectively, subject-specific resources, HTML, and training the public. All staff members (not just librarians) were included in the training program. He also regularly conducted training sessions for the public.

He currently lives in Seattle and works for the Microsoft Corporation.